AFTER

You Get Your Puppy

AFTER
You Get Your Puppy

Dr. Ian Dunbar

James & Kenneth
PUBLISHERS

AFTER You Get Your Puppy
© 2001 Ian Dunbar

First published in 2001 by:

James & Kenneth Publishers
2140 Shattuck Avenue #2406
Berkeley, California 94704
(800) 784-5531

James & Kenneth - Canada
P O Box 14, Palgrave
Ontario LON 1PO
(905) 880-7502

James & Kenneth - UK
P O Box 111, Harpenden
Hertfordshire AL5 2GD
01582 715765

James & Kenneth - OZ
65 Medway Road
Bringelly NSW 2171
02 47 749 324

Printed in the United States of America

IBSN 1-888047-01-1

Dr. Ian Dunbar and Omaha Beagle

Photo Credits
Jennifer Bassing: pages 5, 44, 48, 78, 95
Jamie Dunbar: pages 124, 126, 132
Fisher Houtz: page 25
Mimi WheiPing Lou: page 113
Jennifer Messer: page 145
Carmen Noradunghian: page 110
Sue Pearson: page 26
All other photographs were taken by the author.

Front Cover Illustration by Tracy Dockray
Front Cover Design by Quark & Bark Late Night Graphics Co.
Back Cover Design by Montessaurus Media

Contents

After You Get Your Puppy
Your Puppy's First Three Months at Home

Congratulations! So, you have your new puppy. Now what? Basicall, you are at a fork in the road. The success of the relationship depends on your teaching your puppy the rules and regulations of domestic living. The most critical time in your dog's life is right now - puppyhood! First impressions are indelible and long-lasting. Consequently, the next few weeks are crucially important for your dog's development. Help and guidance at this stage will have a profound and everlasting effect which will enrich the dog-human relationship for many years to come.

BEFORE You Get Your Puppy addressed your puppy's first three developmental deadlines covering 1) your doggy education, 2) the search and selection for a suitable puppy and how to assess its developmental status, and 3) teaching household manners during your puppy's first week at home. The first three developmental deadlines were extremely urgent, crucial, and left precious little room for mistakes. In view of their importance and tight deadline, household manners will be summarized here. *AFTER You Get Your Puppy* will focus on your puppy's next three developmental deadlines during the first three months your puppy is at home.

The clock is still ticking and you only have three months to get a lot of things done.

THE NEXT THREE
DEVELOPMENTAL DEADLINES

4th Developmental Deadline - *by three months of age*
The Most *Urgent* Priority :

Socialization with People

5th Developmental Deadline - *by eighteen weeks of age*
The Most *Important* Priority:

Learning Bite Inhibition

6th Developmental Deadline - *by five months of age*
The Most *Enjoyable* Priority:

Enjoying the World at Large

The Most Urgent Priority is to socialize your puppy to a wide variety of people, especially children, men, and strangers, before it is twelve weeks old. Well-socialized puppies grow up to be wonderful companions, whereas antisocial dogs are difficult, time-consuming, and potentially dangerous. Your puppy needs to learn to enjoy the company of all people and to enjoy being handled by all people, especially children and strangers.

As a rule of thumb, your puppy needs to meet at least a hundred people before it is three months old. Since your puppy is still too young to venture out on the streets, you'll need to start inviting people to your home right away. Basically, you'll need to have lots of Puppy Parties and invite friends over to handfeed your pup and train it for you.

The Most Important Priority is that your puppy learn reliable bite inhibition and develop a soft mouth before it is eighteen weeks old. Whenever a dog bites a person or fights with another dog, the seriousness of the problem depends on the seriousness of the injury. Hence, the ease and success of retraining depends almost entirely on the dog's degree of bite inhibition. The reliability of your dog's bite inhibition determines whether you have a minor problem which may be easily corrected with a few safe, basic training exercises, or whether you have a serious and potentially dangerous problem which is going to be extremely difficult to resolve.

In a perfect world, you will successfully socialize your puppy so that it thoroughly enjoys the company and actions of all people, all dogs, and all animals. More realistically, though, accidents happen. Someone accidentally shuts the dog's tail in the car door. Someone runs to answer the telephone and accidentally treads on a sleeping dog's leg. A child runs and trips and falls on top of the dog while it is gnawing on a bone. When dogs are hurt or startled, their natural response is to snap, lunge, and even bite. Even wonderfully friendly dogs may feel inclined to protect or defend themselves when picked on by other dogs and people.

For example, when hurt or frightened a dog may snap and lunge at a person. But, if it has well-established bite inhibition it is unlikely the dog's teeth will even touch the skin. Or if there is skin contact it is unlikely that the teeth will break the skin. The dog has caused no damage and the potentially serious problem has been easily and safely prevented. If, on the other hand, the dog has inadequate bite inhibition and its teeth puncture the skin, then you have a serious situation which may be difficult and time-consuming to resolve.

Similarly, dogs with well-established bite inhibition never cause damage when fighting with other dogs. The problem is minor because your dog is simply squabbling in a socially acceptable manner. On the other hand, if your dog ever hurts another dog or another animal, you have a major problem and resolution is unlikely.

Bite inhibition *must* be established in puppyhood, before eighteen weeks of age, since it is difficult to instill bite inhibition in an adolescent or adult dog. Learning the skills and techniques to ensure your puppy develops a reliable bite inhibition and an ultra-soft mouth is the primary reason for you to attend off-leash puppy classes. Your puppy needs to play with other puppies. Playing with adult dogs at home or in the park is simply not sufficient.

The Most Enjoyable Priority of dog ownership is to accustom your well-socialized, soft-mouthed puppy to the world at large, thus assuring that it remains well-socialized and soft-mouthed. Remember, your dog will only remain sociable if it continues meeting and greeting unfamiliar people and unfamiliar dogs every day. Meeting the same people and dogs over and over again is not sufficient. You want your dog to practice the art of meeting and getting along with strangers, not simply getting along with old friends. Consequently, regular walks with your dog are as essential as they are enjoyable.

Your life is about to change. You are about to enjoy all the joys of dog ownership - long, energetic, or relaxing walks, trips in the car, afternoons in the dog park, picnics on the beach, plus so many enjoyable organized doggy activities.

Before we address socialization, bite inhibition, and walking your dog, let's review your puppy's household manners.

Household Etiquette 101

It is vital that you have taught your puppy where to eliminate, what to chew, and how to happily enjoy the time when left at home alone. Moreover, it is essential that your puppy's schooling continue forever. If your puppy is having housesoiling or chewing problems, reread *BEFORE You Get Your Puppy* and seek help immediately. Any mistake is a potential disaster because it signals many more mistakes to come. It is important that housetraining and chewtoy-training are errorless. Do not stray from the puppy confinement program. The quicker you housetrain your puppy, the sooner it will get to enjoy free run of your house.

When You Are Not at Home

Keep your puppy confined to a fairly small Puppy Playroom (long-term confinement area), for example, in the kitchen, bathroom, utility room, or section of the room cordoned off by an exercise pen. Include (1) a comfortable bed, (2) a bowl of clean fresh water, (3) plenty of hollow chewtoys (Kong products and sterilized bones stuffed with dog food), and (4) a doggy toilet (in the farthest corner from its bed).

The purpose of a well-designed long-term confinement area is twofold:

1. To prevent mistakes around the house
2. To maximize the likelihood that your puppy will learn to use the provided toilet, only to chew chewtoys (the only chewables available), and settle down calmly and quietly (without barking)

13

Whenever you are away from home, leave your puppy in its playroom. A suitable long-term confinement area needs a waterproof (easy-to-clean) floor, comfortable bed, bowl of fresh water, chewtoys stuffed with kibble, and toilet. If you leave your puppy in the bathroom, remember to put the towels, bath mat, shower curtain, and toilet paper out of reach.

Remember, any housesoiling or chewing mistake is a potential disaster, since it predicts many more to come. If a young (uneducated) puppy is ever allowed unsupervised free run of the house, housesoiling and chewing mistakes are inevitable, and the puppy will more likely become hyperactive and anxious. Confinement prompts the pup to focus on its stuffed chewtoys, leaving it little time to fret, worry, or bark. Of course, once your puppy has mastered household manners and enjoys its time spent at home alone, it may enjoy full run of your house and yard at any time you wish.

When You Are at Home

Supervise your puppy. Or, when the two of you are not play-training, confine your pup for an hour at a time to its Doggy Den (short-term confinement area), such as a portable dog crate. Include (1) a comfortable bed and (2) plenty of stuffed chewtoys.

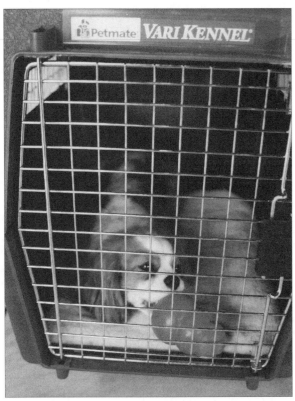

Short-term confinement to a crate has many advantages: It prevents your puppy from making mistakes around the house, maximizes the likelihood the pup will become fixated on chewtoys, and facilitates housetraining, since you may now accurately predict when your puppy needs to relieve itself. If your puppy chews its bed, remove it for a couple of days until the pup has become fixated on chewtoys stuffed with kibble and treats.

The purpose of short-term confinement is threefold:
1. To prevent mistakes around the house
2. To teach your puppy to become a chewtoyaholic (since chewtoys stuffed with food are the only chewables available), so that it learns to settle down quietly and calmly
3. To be able to predict when your puppy needs to eliminate Closely confining a puppy to its bed strongly inhibits urination and defecation, so it will be in dire need to relieve itself when released from the crate each hour.

Being able to accurately predict when your puppy needs to eliminate enables you to be there to teach it where to eliminate, and to reward the pup for doing the right thing in the right place at the right time

---

ℋousetraining is as Easy as 1-2-3

When you are away from home, keep your puppy confined to its Puppy Playroom, where it has a suitable doggy toilet. Otherwise, when you are at home:

1. keep your puppy closely confined to its Doggy Den, or on-leash by its bed;
2. every hour on the hour, release your pup from confinement and quickly run it (on-leash if necessary) to the toilet area. Instruct your pup to eliminate and give it three minutes to do so;
3. enthusiastically praise your puppy, offer it three freeze-dried liver treats, and then play-train indoors or in the yard. Once your puppy is over three months old, take it for a walk as a reward for eliminating in its toilet area.

Common Mistakes

1. Allowing the puppy to make a mistake.

And why did the pup make a mistake? Let's ask its teacher. Who left the puppy with a full rectum and full bladder unattended in the bedroom? Who left the empty puppy unattended to ransack the living room? Who allowed the untrained puppy to be home alone with free run of the house? Please go back and reread the puppy confinement schedule. Your puppy's confinement schedule ensures that your pup's household education continues even when it is left at home alone. Errorless housetraining and chewtoy training is just so simple.

2. Not rewarding the puppy for getting it right.

You didn't praise your pup or offer any tasty treats, and now you wonder why your puppy doesn't do what you want it to do. It is hardly your puppy's fault that it feels free to improvise its doggy toys and toilets. Please go back and reread the puppy confinement schedule. Stuff those chewtoys with kibble and the occasional treat. And always profusely praise and reward your puppy for doing the right thing in the right place at the right time.

Home Alone

At this stage of the game, it is a little late (and largely unprofitable) to snipe, "You shouldn't have gotten a dog if you don't have the time to spend with it." Nonetheless, it is unfair to invite a highly social animal to come and live with you without preparing it to spend some of its time in social isolation and solitary confinement.

All owners find it occasionally necessary to leave their puppydog at home alone. So before leaving your puppy for long periods, you should teach it how to amuse itself appropriately when left alone, such as by chewing stuffed chewtoys, and learning how to enjoy its own company without becoming anxious or stressed.

To teach your puppy how to settle down calmly and quietly when you are absent, start by teaching it to settle down with a chewtoy at times when you are present.

A dog is not like a television or a video game. You can't just pull the plug or temporarily remove the batteries from a rambunctious puppy. Instead, you must teach it to settle down and shush. Right from the outset, make frequent quiet moments part of the puppy's daily routine. Following the above confinement schedule will help your puppy train itself to settle down. Additionally, encourage your puppy to settle down beside you for longer and longer periods. For example, when you're watching television have your pup lie down on leash or in its crate, but release it for short play-training breaks during the commercials. For a young puppy, you can't have too many rules.

When playing with your pup, have it settle down for frequent short interludes every one or two minutes. Initially have the pup lie still for a few seconds before letting it play again. After a minute, interrupt the play session once more with a three-second settle-down. Then try for four seconds, then five, eight, ten, and so on. Although it's difficult at first, being yo-yoed between "Settle Down" and "Let's Play," the puppy soon learns to settle down quickly and happily. Your puppy will learn that "Settle Down" is not the end of the world, nor is it necessarily the end of the play session, but instead that "Settle Down" signals a short time-out and reward-break before being allowed to resume playing.

If you teach your puppy to be calm and controlled when told, you will have years of fun and excitement ahead. Once your puppy has learned to settle down and shush on cue, there is so much more your dog can enjoy with you. Your well-trained dog is likely to be invited for many walks, trips in the car, picnics, visits to the pub, to Grandma's, and even on incredible journeys to stay in ritzy dog-friendly hotels. On the other hand, if you let

Knowing that Claude was an anxious soul and a big-time destructive chewer, for the first ten days after adoption he was fed kibble only from chewtoys placed in his chewtoy basket

your dog play indiscriminately as a puppy, it will no doubt want to play indiscriminately as an adult. Your dog will be hyperactive and uncontrollable because you have taught it to act that way. If your pup has not been taught to settle down by the time it reaches adolescence, it will be unfit to be taken places. Your pup will begin a lifetime of confinement and isolation at home while the rest of the family go out to have a good time. Not fair!

Until you have trained your puppy to enjoy spending much of its day at home alone, you might recruit a puppy sitter who has time to spend with it. Just a few houses down the street, there may live an elderly gentleman, for example, who would just love to live with a dog (but who doesn't for some reason) and therefore would be willing to come over during the daytime and (1) sit and enjoy your TV or the contents of your fridge, (2) maintain your puppy's confinement schedule and regularly reward it for using its doggy toilet, and (3) periodically play with the pup and teach it household rules.

Separation Anxiety

Maintaining your puppy's confinement schedule when you are at home prepares your puppy to be calm when you are gone. Allowing a young puppy unrestricted access to you when you are at home quickly encourages it to become overly dependent, and overdependence is the most common reason why dogs become anxious when left at home alone.

Try your best to teach your puppy to enjoy its own company, to develop self-confidence, and to stand on its own four paws. Once your puppy is confident and relaxed on its own, it may enjoy all of its time with you when you are at home.

When leaving your puppy for hourly sessions in its short-term confinement area (dog crate), make a point to check how it fares when left in another room. For example, periodically confine your puppy to its crate in the dining room while you prepare food in the kitchen, then keep the pup in its crate in the kitchen while the family eats dinner in the dining room. Most importantly, when you are at home, make certain to familiarize your puppy with his long-term confinement area (puppy playroom). Confining your pup when you're home enables you to monitor its behavior during confinement and check in on it at irregular intervals, quietly rewarding it for being quiet. Thus, your pup will not necessarily associate its confinement area with your absence, but rather it will learn to look forward to time spent in its playroom with its special toys.

Give your puppy plenty of toys whenever leaving it on its own. Ideal chewtoys are indestructible and hollow (such as Kong products or sterilized longbones), as they may be conveniently stuffed with kibble and occasional treats which

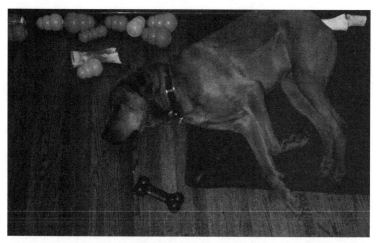

Claude Konged - peacefully passing the time when left at home alone
(after chewing himself to sleep).

periodically fall out and reward the pup for chewing its toy. If your puppy is gainfully occupied with its chewtoy, it will fret less over your absence. Additionally, leave a radio playing. The sound will provide white noise to mask outside disturbances. Also, the sound of a radio is reassuring, since it is normally associated with your presence. My Malamute Phoenix is quite partial to classical music, country, and calypso. Oso prefers television, especially ESPN or CNN – the sound of trustworthy male voices perhaps?

When Leaving Home

Make sure to stuff a number of chewtoys with kibble and treats. Make sure to stuff a piece of freeze-dried liver into the tiny hole of each Kong, or deep into the marrow cavity of each bone. Place the tastily stuffed chewtoys in your puppy's long-term confinement area and shut the door . . . with your puppy on the outside! When your puppy begs you to open the door, let it in and shut the door, turn on the radio or television, and leave quietly. Your puppy's chewing will be regularly reinforced by each piece of kibble which falls out of the chewtoy. Your puppy will continue to chew in an attempt to extract the freeze-dried liver. Eventually your puppy will fall asleep.

When Returning Home

Do not acknowledge your puppy's presence with praise or petting until it retrieves a chewtoy. Once it brings you a chewtoy, use a pen or pencil to push out the piece of freeze-dried liver which your puppy has been unable to extract. This will impress your puppy to no end.

Dogs are crepuscular and quite happy to sleep all day and all night. They have two activity peaks, at dawn and dusk. Thus, most chewing and barking activity is likely to occur right after you leave your pup in the morning and just before you return in the evening. Leaving your puppy with freshly stuffed chewtoys and offering the unextracted treats when you return prompts your puppy to seek out its chewtoys at times of peak activity.

Jekyll and Hyde Behavior

Smothering your puppy with attention and affection when you are home primes the pup to really miss you when you are gone. A Jekyll and Hyde environment (lots of attention when your are there and none when you are gone) quickly creates a Jeckyl and Hyde puppy which is completely confident when you are there, but falls apart and panics when you are gone.

If you allow your puppy to become dependent upon your presence, it will be anxious in your absence. Canine anxiety is bad news for you and bad news for your pup. When stressed,

---

Wonderful Weekends - Worrisome Weekdays!

Whereas weekend attention and affection is wonderful, it primes your new puppy to miss the family on Monday morning when the parents go to work and the children leave for school. By all means, play-train with your puppy lots during the weekend, but also have lots of quiet moments to prepare your puppy for lonely weekdays.

Many supposed signs of separation anxiety are really signs of an insufficiently trained dog being allowed unsupervised free range of the house and encountering temptation left by their owners.

dogs are more likely to indulge in bad habits, such as housesoiling, chewing digging, and barking. Being anxious is also decidedly unpleasant for your dog.

During your puppy's first few weeks at home, frequent confinement with stuffed chewtoys is essential for your pup to develop confidence and independence. Once your puppy is quite happy busying itself with its chewtoys whenever left alone, you may safely allow your now well-behaved and confident pup to enjoy as much time with you as it likes, without the fear that it will become anxious in your absence.

Separation Anxiety?

Most doggy "disobedience" and wanton house destruction occurring in the owner's absence has nothing to do with separation anxiety. In fact, separation relief might be a more precise and descriptive term. The dog chews, digs, barks, and soils the house only when the owner is absent because it has learned it would be foolhardy to indulge in these pastimes when the owner is present. Owner-absent misbehavior is an indication that the owner has tried to suppress normal and natural dog behaviors with punishment, rather than teaching the dog how to behave, namely, how to express its basic doggy desires in an acceptable fashion. Often the term separation anxiety is an excuse for a dog who is simply not yet housetrained or chewtoy-trained.

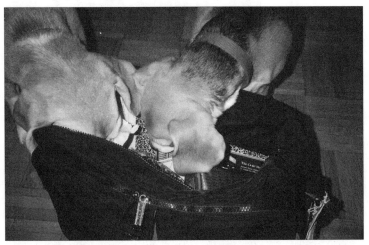

Beagles just begging to "unpack" a visitor's unattended luggage.

4th DEVELOPMENTAL DEADLINE
By Three Months of Age

Socialization with People

Raising and training a pup to be people-friendly is the second most important goal of pet dog husbandry. Teaching bite inhibition is always the most important goal of development. But during your pup's first month at home, urgency dictates that Socialization with People is the Prime Puppy Directive.

Your puppy must be fully socialized to people before it is three months old. Many people think puppy classes are the time to socialize puppies to people. Not so. Too little, much too late. Puppy classes are a fun night out (1) to continue socializing socialized puppies with people, (2) for therapeutic socialization of puppies with other puppies, and most importantly, (3) for puppies to learn bite inhibition.

You now have just a few weeks left to socialize your puppy. Unfortunately, your pup needs to be confined indoors until it is at least three months old, i.e., until it has acquired sufficient immunity (via its puppy shots) against the more serious dog diseases. However, even a relatively short period of social isolation at such a crucial developmental stage could all but ruin your puppy's temperament. Whereas dog-dog socialization may be put on temporary hold until your pup is old enough to go to puppy school and the dog park, you simply can not delay socialization with people. It may be possible to live with a dog that does not like other dogs, but it is difficult and potentially dangerous to live with a dog that does not like people, especially if the dog doesn't like some of your friends and family.

Consequently, there is considerable urgency to introduce your puppy to a wide variety of people–to family, friends, and strangers and especially to men, and children. As a rule of thumb, your pup needs to meet at least a hundred different people before it is three months old, (an average of three new people a day).

Urgency

From the very first day you get your puppy, the clock is ticking, and time flies! By eight weeks of age, your puppy's Critical Period of Socialization is already waning and within a month, its most impressionable learning period will start to close. There is so much to teach, and nearly everything needs to be taught right away.

Puppies may become infected with serious puppy diseases by sniffing the urine or feces of infected dogs. Never let your puppy be on the ground where other dogs may have eliminated. You may take your puppy for car rides and to visit friends but always carry your puppy from house to car and vice versa. Of course, these precautions also apply to visits to the veterinary clinic. The ground immediately outside the door of the clinic and the floor of the waiting room are two of the most likely contaminated areas. Carry your puppy from the car to the clinic and keep it on your lap in the waiting room. Better yet, keep your puppy crated in your car until it is time for its examination.

Doggy Dream or Nasty Nightmare?

The most important quality in a pet dog is its temperament. A dog with a good temperament can be a dream to live with, but a dog with a tricky temperament is a perpetual nightmare. Moreover, regardless of breed or breeding, a dog's temperament, especially its feelings towards people and other dogs, is primarily the result of socialization (or lack of socialization) during puppyhood, the most important time in a dog's life. Do not waste this golden opportunity. Solid gold temperaments are forged during this period.

A Hundred People!

Capitalize on the time your pup needs to be confined indoors by inviting people to your home. Your pup needs to socialize with at least a hundred different people before it is three months old. This is actually quite easy to accomplish. Twice a week, invite

Not a bad start. Eighteen people to meet one three-month-old puppy at home.

different groups of six men to watch sports on TV. Generally, men are pretty easy to attract if you offer television sports programs, pizza, and beer. On several other nights a week, invite different groups of six women for ice cream, chocolate, and good conversation. On another night of the week, catch up on all of your outstanding social obligations by inviting family, friends, and neighbors for Meet-the-Puppy dinners. And, have a Puppy Party once a week. Above all, don't keep your puppy a secret. One of the great things about puppy socialization is that it also does wonders for your social life!

Sample Invitation

Mr. Nice Guy

is cordially invited to a

Meet-the-Puppy Party

7:30-9:00pm - March 7th

Please come and help my puppy learn to love men.

Healthy gourmet food, premium beverages,

and televised sports will be provided.

Please bring an additional adult male human.

R.S.V.P. (510) 555-1234

Three Goals of Socialization

1. The first step is to teach your puppy to enjoy the presence, actions, and antics of all people, first the family and then friends and strangers, especially children and men. Adult dogs tend to feel most uneasy around children and men, especially around little boys. A dog's antipathy toward children and men is more likely to develop if the puppy grows up with few or no children or men around, and if the puppy's social contacts with children and men have been unpleasant or scary.

2. Teach your puppy to enjoy being hugged and handled (restrained and examined) by people, especially by children, veterinarians, and groomers. Specifically, teach your puppy to enjoy being touched and handled in a variety of "hot spots," namely, around its collar, ears, paws, muzzle, tail, and rear end.

3. Teach your puppy to enjoy giving up valued objects when requested, especially its food bowl, bones, balls, chewtoys, garbage, and paper tissues.

1. Teach Your Puppy to Like and Respect People

Compensate for your puppy's temporary but necessary social vacuum during its first month at home by introducing it to as many people as possible in the safety of its own home. Initial impressions are important, so make sure your puppy's first meetings with people are pleasant and enjoyable. Have every guest handfeed your puppy a couple of pieces of kibble. Puppies who enjoy the company of people grow up into adult dogs who enjoy the company of people. And dogs who enjoy the company of people are less likely to be frightened or bite.

Make sure to invite a number of different people to your home each day. It is not sufficient for your pup to meet the same people over and over again. Your puppy needs to grow accustomed to meeting strangers, at least three a day. Maintain routine hygiene at all times; have guests leave outdoor shoes outside and wash their hands before handling your puppy.

Teaching your puppy to perform friendly (playful and appeasing) behaviors on cue helps people to feel good about your dog, and helps your dog to feel good about people.

Training Treats?

To prevent your puppy from pigging out on junk food treats, use your pup's daily ration of kibble as training treats. To prevent your puppy from being overfed by members of the family, first thing in the morning measure your puppy's daily diet of kibble plus treats into a separate container. Thus, at any time of the day, if any kibble or treats remain in the container they may be fed to the puppy as a snack, as a meal, or individually hand-fed as rewards when training.

Give every guest a bag of training treats, so that your puppy will be inclined to like them from the outset. Show your guests how you use your puppy's dinner kibble to lure/reward train it to come, sit, lie down, and roll over. Ask your puppy to come. Praise it profusely as it approaches and give it a piece of kibble when it arrives. Back up and do it again. Repeat the sequence several times.

In dog language, a play bow means "I am friendly and want to play," and raising a paw (shaking hands) means "I respect your higher rank and want to be friends."

Each time it approaches, have the puppy sit. Say, "Puppy Sit," and slowly move a piece of kibble upwards, from in front of its nose to between its eyes. As the puppy raises its nose to sniff the kibble, it will lower its rear end and sit. If the puppy jumps up, you are holding the food lure too high, and so repeat the procedure with the food closer to the pup's muzzle. When your puppy sits, say, "Good Dog," and give it the kibble.

Now have the puppy come, sit, and lie down. Once the pup sits, say, "Puppy Down," and lower a piece of kibble from just in front of its nose to between its forepaws. As the puppy lowers its head to follow the food, it will usually lie down. Don't worry if your puppy stands instead, just keep the kibble hidden under the palm of your hand until it lies down. As soon as it does so, say, "Good Dog," and give it the food.

Now teach your guests how to train your pup to rollover. Once the pup is lying down, say, "Puppy Rollover," and move the kibble from in front of its nose to its shoulder blade and slowly over its backbone. Once the puppy rolls over onto its back, say, "Good Dog," and give it the kibble.

When successfully lure/rewarded to come, sit, and lie down, your puppydog demonstrates voluntary compliance and respect for your wishes (whether requests, instructions, or commands). There is absolutely no need to force or bully a dog to get it to show respect.

Repeat the come here, sit, down, and rollover sequence until the puppy responds reliably, and then help each guest practice these maneuvers until each one can get the puppy to come, sit, lie down, and rollover three times in succession for a single piece of kibble.

If your puppy is regularly hand-fed dinner by guests in this manner, it will soon learn to enjoy the company of people and to approach happily and sit automatically when greeting them. And, of course, as an added bonus you will have successfully trained your family and friends to help you train your puppy.

Willing Compliance

*When a puppydog approaches promptly and happily, it is a sure sign that it is people-friendly.

*Sitting and lying down in close proximity to people further shows that your dog likes them. Using food lures and rewards in training is the best possible way to teach your dog to like children and strangers.

*A puppy that has been taught by a range of people to lie down and rollover will have learned to show friendly appeasement and deference upon request.

*Most importantly, by coming, sitting, lying down, and rolling over on request, your dog shows respect for the person issuing instructions. This is especially important with children. When children lure/reward train, they issue requests (commands), and the dog happily and voluntarily complies (obeys). And when it comes to dogs and children, happy and voluntary compliance is the only type of compliance that is effective and safe.

Children

The actions and antics of children can be extremely scary to adults dogs which were not socialized with children during puppyhood. Even well-socialized adult dogs may get into trouble, since much that children do excites dogs and incites them to play and chase. Puppies and children must be taught how to behave around each other. This is easy and fun to do, so let's do it.

Even playful hugging may be scary for an unsocialized puppy, and would be unlikely to be tolerated by the dog in adulthood

For puppy owners with children, the next few months present a bit of a challenge. However, it is infinitely worthwhile because puppies successfully socialized with children generally develop exceedingly sound temperaments (they have to), and once they mature there is little in life that can surprise or upset them. However, to maximize the relationship between dogs and children and to ensure your dog's good nature and solid disposition, parents must educate their children as well as the pup. Teach your children how to act around the pup, and teach your pup how to act around children.

Puppy owners without children have a different kind of challenge. You must invite children to your home to meet your puppy now! However, unless your child training skills exceed your puppy training skills, initially invite over children only in small numbers. To start with, invite only a single child. One child is marvelous. Two are fine. But usually, three children plus a puppy quickly reach critical mass and emit levels of energy, unmeasurable by any known scientific instrument. And, after all, we are trying to teach the puppy and the children to be calm and mannerly.

Children and puppies (or dogs) should never be left together unsupervised.

First, invite over only well-trained children. Supervise the children at all times. I repeat, supervise the children at all times. (Later on, puppy classes will offer a wonderful source of

With appropriate guidance and constant supervision, many children may become wonderful dog trainers.

children who have been trained how to act around puppies and who have been trained how to train puppies.)

Second, invite over your friends' and relatives' children - children your puppy is likely to meet on a regular or occasional basis when it is an adult.

Third, invite over neighborhood children. Remember, it is usually neighborhood kids who would terrorize your dog through the garden fence, exciting it and inciting it to bark, growl, snap, and lunge. Then, of course, it is the children's parents (your neighbors) who complain because your dog is barking and harassing their kids. Dogs are less likely to bark at children they know and like, so give your puppy ample opportunity to get to know and like neighborhood children. Similarly, children are less likely to tease a dog they know and like owned by people they know and like, so give the neighborhood kids ample opportunity to get to know and like you and your puppy.

Make a point to give children tasty treats (freeze-dried liver) as well as kibble to use as lures and rewards during handling

By coming when called and sitting on request, a puppy demonstrates willing compliance and shows respect to its trainer – a child.

and training exercises. Thus, your puppy will quickly learn to love the presence and presents of children.

For the first week, make sure your puppy's interactions with children are carefully controlled and calm. Thereafter, however, it is important for Puppy Parties to be festive. Balloons, streamers, and music set the stage, and treats for the puppies plus presents, noise-makers and, glucose for the children, set the scene.

It is so important that your puppy is very young when it first encounters and becomes thoroughly accustomed to the noise and activity of children. If your dog is already an adolescent before he sees his first child running and screaming in the park, generally you will be in for trouble for the dog will want to give chase. However, for the lucky puppy who has hosted numerous Puppy Parties, with children (or adults) laughing, screaming, running, skipping, and falling over . . . well, that's just old hat. Been there, done that! After just a couple of occasions partying with children, it is unlikely anything in real life will be as weird as what has become the snoring-boring, established status quo during Puppy Parties.

Puppy Party Games

Initially, Round Robin Recalls and Puppy Push-ups are the best games to play. Have the children sit in chairs in a big circle. The first child calls the puppy and has it lie down and sit up three times in succession before sending it to the next child in the circle – "Rover Go To Jamie", whereupon Jamie calls the puppy to come and perform three puppy push-ups and so on. This is a wonderful exercise to practice prompt recalls and lightning-fast control commands (sits and downs).

Callahan learns Bang! (a Down-Stay).

In subsequent Puppy Parties, Biscuit Balance and Drop Dead Dog competitions are the name of the game. Give each child praise and a prize, but give special praise and special prizes to the children who can get the dog to balance a MilkBone on its nose for the longest time, that is, the longest Sit-Stay, or to get the dog to lie down and play dead for the longest time, i.e., the longest Down-Stay.

As a rule of thumb, before your puppy is three months old it needs to have been handled and trained (to come, sit, lie down, and rollover) by at least twenty children.

Doug, a child at heart, teaches Skooter to balance a Milk Bone on his head, and Skooter has fun learning a Sit-Stay.

Men

Many adult dogs are more fearful of men than they are of women. So invite over as many men as possible to handle and gentle your puppy. It is especially important to invite men to socialize with your puppy if no men are living in the household. Make sure you teach all male visitors how to handfeed kibble to lure/reward your pup to come, sit, lie down, and rollover. Add a few extra tasty treats to each male visitor's bag of training kibble so that your puppy forms a fond and loving bond with men.

Chihuahua puppy cuddle time.

Strangers

Young puppies tend to be universally accepting and tolerant of all people, but, unless taught otherwise, adolescent and adult dogs predictably develop a natural wariness of people they do not know. Introducing your puppy to a hundred people before it is three months old will help make it more accepting of strangers as an adolescent. However, in order for your adult dog to remain continually accepting of strangers, it needs to continually meet strangers. Meeting the same people over and over just won't do it. Your adult dog needs to meet new people each day, so you must maintain your newly improved social life at home and/or walk your dog regularly.

Sit to Say Hello

As early as possible, establish sitting as the status quo for greeting people. Make sure each family member, visitor, or stranger has the puppy sit before they say hello, praise, pet, or offer a food reward. In no time, your puppy will learn to sit automatically when people approach. Sitting for praise or a food reward when greeting people certainly beats jumping up. And from the dog's viewpoint, sitting for attention, affection, and treats certainly beats getting punished for jumping up!

Warning!

If your puppy is slow to approach, or doesn't approach your guests, do something about it now. Certainly your puppy may be shy, but also it is frighteningly under-socialized. It is absolutely abnormal for a two- to three-month-old puppy not to eagerly approach people. You must resolve this problem within one week; otherwise, it will rapidly get worse - much worse. Moreover, if you let the days slip by, future attempts at therapeutic socialization will become progressively less effective. Please do not ignore your puppy's fears by rationalizing, "He takes a while to warm to strangers." If your pup takes a while to warm to strangers now, it will likely be intolerant and scared of strangers as an adult. It is simply not fair to let your puppy grow up to be scared and anxious around people. Please help your puppy today.

The solution is simple and effective, and usually only takes one week. For the next seven days, invite over half a dozen different people each day to handfeed your puppy's meals. For just one week, your puppy must not receive any food from family members or in its dog bowl. This technique works quickly if your puppy only receives kibble and treats from the hands of household guests. Once the puppy happily accepts food from the hand, your guests may then ask the pup to come, sit, and lie down for each piece of kibble. Your guests will soon become your puppy's new best friends.

Teasing and Roughhousing

Children and men especially appear to enjoy teasing, manhandling, or roughhousing with puppies. Puppies may find teasing and roughhousing to be positive and enjoyable, or unpleasant and frightening.

Good-natured teasing can be a lot of fun for both parties. Properly done, teasing can do a lot to build a puppy's confidence by gradually and progressively desensitizing it to all

---

A Very Important Rule

A single person can have a dramatic impact on your puppy's personality - for better or worse. Insist that nobody (NOBODY) interacts or plays with your puppy until they demonstrate they can get it to come eagerly, sit promptly, and lie down calmly.

Untrained visitors, especially children and adult male friends and relatives, are renowned for ruining good puppies in short order. If your visitors won't listen and wise up, put your puppy in its long-term confinement area, or ask the visitors to leave.

---

the weird things that men and children do. On the other hand, relentless teasing can be frustrating and damaging. Malicious teasing is not teasing; it is abuse.

Confidence-building might involve temporarily withholding toys or treats from the pup, temporarily hugging or restraining the pup, making strange noises, or temporarily making mildly scary faces or slightly weird body movements, and then praising the pup and offering a food treat. The food reward builds the puppy's confidence by reinforcing its acceptance of your scary faces and weird actions. With each repetition you

Roughhousing can be scary for puppies, and playfighting is a common cause for owners' lack of control over their dogs. On the other hand, with just a little common sense, roughhousing and playfighting can be the very best confidence-building, bite inhibition, and control exercises. Have frequent time-outs to calm, praise, and reassure your pup. Whenever your puppy's needle-sharp teeth cause pain, yelp! Ignore your puppy for thirty seconds or so and then instruct it to come, sit, and lie down before resuming play. Make sure you have frequent training interludes to check that you can still control your puppy and instantly get it to stop playing, to sit, lie down, and calm down

may act a little scarier and weirder before offering a treat. After time, your puppy will confidently accept any human action or mannerism. If the puppy ever refuses a treat, you have stressed it. So stop being silly for while until you have handfeed the pup half a dozen treats in a non-threatening situation. Puppies have to be trained to enjoy relentless teasing. For example, being relentlessly pursued by a child with outstretched arms can be the scariest thing on the planet for a puppy without prior preparation. However, being pursued round the dining room table by an owner doing monster-walks can be one of the most enjoyable games for a puppy who has been patiently taught to enjoy playing the game. Most dogs love to be chased as long as they have been taught that the game is non-threatening.

Malicious teasing - taking pleasure in the puppy's displeasure - is just too cruel and silly for words. It is decidedly not funny to cause the puppy discomfort or to make it afraid. You are teaching the pup to distrust people, and it is your fault when, as an adult, the dog reacts defensively. Sadly though, it will be the dog that gets into trouble, not you. Please don't.

There is a simple test to determine whether or not the puppy finds teasing to be enjoyable. Stop the game, back up, and ask the puppy to come and sit. If the puppy comes promptly with a wagging tail and sits with its head held high, it is probably enjoying the game as much as you are. You may continue playing. If the pup approaches with a wiggly body, lowered head and tail, makes excessive licking motions with its tongue, and lies down or rolls over when asked to sit, you have pushed the puppy too far and it no longer trusts you. Stop playing and rebuild the puppy's confidence by repeatedly backing up and asking the pup to come and sit for a piece of kibble. If the puppy is slow to approach or doesn't come when called, it doesn't like you any more than it likes the evil game you're playing. Stop playing immediately. Take a long look in a mirror. Reflect on what you've done. Then go back and repair the damage by tossing food treats to the puppy until you can get it to confidently and happily come and sit three times in a row.

Because teasing may be beneficial or detrimental, you must regularly and repeatedly test that your puppy is having a good time. Check that the pup will come and sit before starting the game, and stop the game at least once a minute to see if will still do so. This is a sensible precaution anyway, to check that you are still in control of the puppy, even when it is excited and having fun.

Similarly, make sure that your family and friends all demonstrate the same ability to get the pup to come, sit, lie down, and rollover before allowing them to play with your puppy. This simple and effective precaution should apply to men, women, and children.

When played intelligently, physical games, such as play-fighting and tug-of-war, are effective bite inhibition and control exercises, which are wonderful for motivating adult dogs

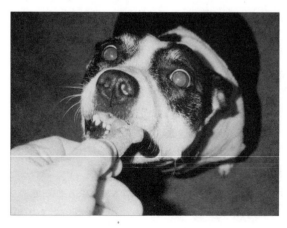

during obedience training. However, in order to be effective and not produce out-of-control dogs, these games must be played according to strict rules, the most important being: You are in control at all times, thata is, at any time you are able to get your puppy to stop playing and lie down calmly with a single "Down" command. If you do not have this level of control, do not roughhouse with your puppy; you'll ruin it so quickly. If, on the other hand, you would like to play physical games with your puppy, I suggest you read the *Preventing Aggression* Behavior Booklet.

Handfeeding

1. Handfeeding teaches your puppy to like kibble, which may then be used effectively as lures and rewards for handling and gentling exercises and for basic training, especially by children, men, and strangers.

2. Handfeeding teaches your puppy to like training and its trainers, especially children, men, and strangers.

3. Teaching your puppy "Off" and "Take it" will help prevent it from becomming a food guarder.

4. Teaching your puppy to "Take it . . . Gently" is the very core of your puppy's developing a soft mouth and learning bite inhibition.

5. Handfeeding enables you to choose convenient times for teaching your pup to control its jaws, rather than having to deal with your puppy whenever it decides to play-bite and bother you.

2. Handling and Gentling

Living with and loving a dog you cannot touch, cuddle, or hug is just about as silly as living with and loving a person you cannot hug. It is also potentially dangerous. Even so, veterinarians and groomers will tell you that hard-to-handle dogs are extremely common. Indeed, many dogs are extremely

stressed when restrained and/or examined by strangers. There are few physical differences between hugging and restraint, or between being handling and examination. The difference depends on your puppy's perspective. Generally, puppies feel they are hugged and handled by friends, but restrained and examined by strangers.

Veterinarians and groomers simply cannot do their job unless your dog remains relaxed and still while being

What's the point of living with a dog if it doesn't like being handled or hugged?

examined. Fearful and aggressive adult dogs and sometimes just plain wriggly adolescent dogs often need to be restrained, tranquilized, or even anesthetized for routine physical examination, teeth-cleaning, and grooming. Restraint makes the procedure much scarier for dogs. Untrained dogs are exposed to the risk of anesthesia, and the additional safety precautions consume the veterinarians' time, and hence costs the owners more money. It is just too silly: Adult humans do not require anesthesia during routine trips to the doctor, dentist, and hair dresser; neither would dogs, if only their owners had taught them to enjoy meeting and being handled by people.

It is simply not fair to allow your puppy to grow up to be wary and anxious around people and afraid of their touch. It is cruel to invite an ultra-social animal to live in the world of humans, yet neglect to teach it to enjoy human company and contact. The poor dog is subjected to a lifetime of psychological torture, which in many ways is worse than other kinds of abuse.

It is not sufficient that your pup merely tolerates handling; it must learn to thoroughly enjoy being handled by strangers. A dog that doesn't thoroughly enjoy being restrained and examined by strangers is a time bomb waiting to go off. One day an unfamiliar child will attempt to hug and pet your dog. Your dog may object. Then the child, you, and your dog all have a big problem.

Your puppy needs to be handled by (1) familiar people before unfamiliar people, (2) adults before children, (3) women before men, and (4) girls before boys.

As with the socialization exercises, adult family members need to accustom the pup to enjoy being handled and gently restrained, so that your puppy knows and enjoys the handling and gentling game before strangers and children become involved. It is quite easy - and thoroughly enjoyable - to teach young puppies to like being handled and examined by people, whereas teaching adolescent and adult dogs to accept handling, especially by children and strangers, can be time-consuming and potentially dangerous. So do not delay. Do it now.

ℋ*ugging* / ℛ*estraint*

This is the fun part: You get to hug your puppy. In fact every family member and all your guests get to hug the puppy. Relaxing with your puppy is a lot of fun, especially if your puppy is relaxed. If it is not relaxed, you are going to teach your puppy to relax, calm down, and thoroughly enjoy a good long cuddle.

Provided your pup was handled frequently prior to weaning and especially neonatally, at eight weeks of age it should go as limp as a noodle whenever picked up and settle down as relaxed as a rag doll on your lap. Even if your puppy did not have the benefit of plentiful early handling in its original

Before starting specific handling exercises, make sure that your puppy is perfectly relaxed lying in your lap. Once your puppy trusts you and has developed sufficient confidence, it will happily snuggle and flop as loose as a rag doll.

home, handling exercises are easy at eight weeks of age. However, you had better get started, because in just twelve weeks time, with a hard-to-handle five-month-old adolescent, the same simple handling exercises will be a completely different story. Untrained adolescent dogs are notoriously difficult to handle.

Pick up your pup, put it on your lap, and hook one finger around its collar so that it doesn't jump off. Slowly and repetitively stroke the pup along the top of its head and back in an attempt to get it to settle down in any position it finds comfortable. If your pup is a bit squirrelly and squirmy, soothingly massage its chest or the base of its ears. Once the pup is completely relaxed, pick up the pup and lay it down on its back for a soothing tummy rub. Massage its belly by making a repetitive circular motion with the palm of your hand. Gently rubbing the pup's inguinal area (where the inside of the thigh joins the abdomen) will also help the puppy relax. While your puppy is calm and relaxed, periodically pick it up to give it a short hug. Gradually and progressively increase the length of the hugs (restraint). After a while, pass the puppy to someone else and have them repeat the above exercises.

Calming Quickly

In addition to lengthy periods of massage and occasional hugs, see how quickly you can get your pup to calm down. Alternate short play sessions with periods of calming down and gentle restraint. Once the puppy calms down quickly in your lap, try getting it to calm down on the floor.

Tantrums?

Should your pup struggle violently, or especially if it has a tantrum, you must not let go. Otherwise your puppy will learn that if it struggles or throws a tantrum, it needn't calm down and be handled because the owner gives in. Bad news! With one hand on your pup's collar and the palm of your other hand against the puppy's chest, gently but firmly hold the pup's back against your abdomen. Hold the puppy so that its four legs point away from you and sufficiently lowdown against your abdomen so that it can not turn its head and bite your face. Hold the pup until it calms down, which it will eventually do. Continue massaging the pups ear with the fingers of one hand and its chest with the fingertips of your other hand. As soon as the puppy calms down and stops struggling, praise the pup, and after a few seconds of calm let it go. Then repeat the procedure.

If you have difficulty getting the pup to calm down and enjoy being hugged (restrained) after one day of practice, call a trainer to your home immediately. This is an emergency. You do not want to live with a dog you can not handle or hug. Call The Association of Pet Dog Trainers at 1-800 PET DOGS to locate a suitable trainer in your area.

Alpha Rollover???

Your puppy will not trust and respect you if manhandled and forciby restrained on its back. It will become more resistant. You'll soon have a puppy that doesn't even enjoy being cuddled because it perceives your hugs as forcible restraint. Be gentle and patient as described above.

Handling / Examination

Teaching your eight-week-old puppy to enjoy being handled and examined is as easy as it is essential. Moreover, your pup's veterinarian, trainer, and groomer will be forever grateful, as will you and your puppy will be. It is a truly unfortunate puppy that finds it scary to be handled and examined.

Many dogs have a number of "hotspots," which if not defused in puppyhood can be extremely sensitive to touch. Handling the ears, paws, muzzle, collar area, and rear end often

provokes a defensive reaction in an adult dog if these areas have not been desensitized during puppyhood. Similarly, an adult dog may act fearfully or defensively when you stare into its eyes, if as a puppy it was not taught to enjoy direct eye-contact.

Some areas become sensitive over time simply because nobody bothers to examine

them. For example, few owners regularly inspect their dog's rear end, or open its mouth to examine the teeth. Some areas are naturally sensitive and may provoke a reaction even in puppies. For example, nearly every puppy will bite your hand if you firmly take hold of its leg or paw. Other areas become sensitive because of bad husbandry and mishandling. Dogs with hangy-down ears, which are prone to infection, soon

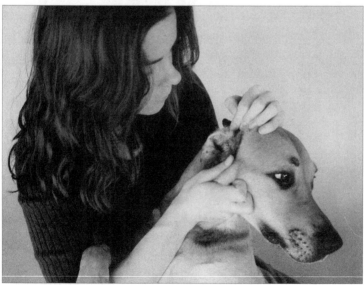

Make sure your puppy feels totally at ease when you handle and examine its ears, muzzle, teeth, and paws. Handfeed your puppy a lot of kibble as you examine each specific area.

come to associate ear examinations with pain. Similarly, many adult dogs associate being stared at or being grabbed by the collar with bad times. Dogs quickly become handshy when people take them by the collar to lead them to confinement, grab them by the collar to put them on leash (thus ending an otherwise enjoyable play session in the park), or grab them by the dog collar to punish them for some transgression.

Handling and examination exercises serve to defuse the hotspots and help the puppy form positive associations with being handled. Desensitizing the puppy and teaching it to enjoy handling is simple when combined with handfeeding it kibble. So simple in fact that it is surprising there are so many hard-to-handle adult dogs.

Please remember that your puppy has two ears and four paws!
Many veterinarians and groomers get quite a shock examining the second ear or the hind paws, when the owner has practiced handling only one ear (usually the dog's right ear with the right hand) and only the front paws.

It is easy to teach your puppy to enjoy being handled. Use your puppy's daily allotment of kibble as training treats. Take hold of your pup's collar and offer a treat. Gaze into your pup's eyes and offer a treat. Look in one ear and offer a treat. Look in the other ear and offer another treat. Hold a paw and offer a treat. Repeat with each paw. Open its mouth and offer a treat. Feel its rear end and private parts and offer a treat. And then repeat the sequence. Each time you repeat the process, progressively handle and examine each area more thoroughly and for longer periods.

Once your puppy is quite happy being handled and examined by family members, it is time to play Pass the Puppy with your guests. One at a time, have each guest offer the pup a treat, take hold of its collar, look in its eyes, handle and examine its ears, paws, teeth, and rear end, and offer treats as described above before passing the pup (plus the bag of dinner kibble) to the next person.

Few people intend to hurt or frighten a puppy, but accidents happen. For example, a guest may inadvertently step on its paw, or the owner might accidentally grab its hair when reaching for the collar. But if the pup feels secure when being handled, it will be less likely to react defensively.

There are two undeniable facts about punishment:
1. any punishment for inappropriate behavior is an advertisement that you have yet to effectively teach your dog how you would like it to act; and
2. in most cases, the dog associates punishment with the trainer and the training situation, understandably causing it to dislike both training and trainer.

Punishment

Insufficient socialization and frequent and extreme punishment are the two major reasons why dogs become wary of people. Many dogs stay away from people. Problems happen when people approach and try to handle, or pet, the dog. Few people intend to make things unpleasant for their puppydog, with one notable exception: when punishing it. By definition, punishment is meant to be unpleasant. However, it is extremely disturbing that this unpleasantness is overly frequent and overly extreme. Sadly, many outdated trainers, and hence many owners who have read outdated training books, tend to focus on punishing untrained dogs for getting it wrong, (i.e., breaking rules they never knew existed). It is much quicker to teach your puppy the rules of the house – to show it what you want it to do and to reward it for doing it. Thus, your puppy learns to want to do what you want it to do. Frequent and/or extreme punishment is a major reason why many dogs dislike being handled, and why they dislike the handler.

Frequent Punishment is an indication that your training philosophy is flawed. The dog still frequently misbehaves and, therefore is frequently punished. Training is simply not working. Time to change to Plan B. Rather than punishing your puppy for mistakes it has made in the past, you should concentrate on teaching your puppy how it should act in the future. Remember, it is much more efficient and effective to reward your puppy for doing it your way - the one way you consider to be right - rather than trying to punish it for the many ways it could do it wrong.

Repeated punishment is the painful tip of the wedge which progressively divides and destroys the pet-owner relationship. Initially, you will lose off-leash control, your dog will be slow to approach (since it no longer wants to come close), and eventually it will become wary and apprehensive when approached and handled. The whole point of living with a dog is to enjoy its company. Surely you don't want to live with a dog that doesn't want your companionship. If you find yourself frequently reprimanding and punishing your puppy, seek help from a trainer.

Extreme Punishment is an extreme indication that training isn't working. The dog still misbehaves and the severity of punishment is increased with the assumption that it will be more effective. If punishment is effective, the dog would no longer misbehave. If the dog continues to misbehave following an extreme punishment, it would be wise to question the validity of the punishment-training program rather than automatically upping the level of pain. Extreme punishment is quite unnecessary and absolutely counterproductive. It creates more problems than it resolves. Even when extreme punishment is effective in eliminating unwanted behavior, it trashes the dog-human relationship. For example, your puppy may not jump up anymore following a severe punishment, but now he no longer likes you, nor wants to come close to you; you were extremely nasty to him the last time he jumped up to say hello. You have won the battle but lost the war. Your dog doesn't jump up, but you don't have a best friend anymore. Sadly, training has become adversarial and unpleasant. Why would a person treat their best friend like their worst enemy?

For goodness sake, if you ever feel the need to resort to severe punishment, immediately seek help from a trainer who uses more efficient and effective, dog-friendly, lure/reward training methods. The most successful obedience competition dogs, agility dogs, search and rescue dogs, bomb detection dogs, seeing-eye dogs, hearing-ear dogs, assistance dogs, and protection dogs are all trained using reward-based motivational methods, with few if any reprimands. Isn't it about time that we trained pet dogs the same way? When effectively using reward-training techniques, punishment is seldom necessary. However, a less-experienced trainer may feel the need to reprimand or punish more frequently in order to compensate for their novice training skills. Even so, when punishing a dog there is no need to approach, loom over, glower, grab, shake, shout, scream, scare, or hurt it.

For a routine training mishap, an instructive reprimand is more than sufficient, such as, "Outside!", "Chewtoy!", "Sit!", "Steady!", or "Hustle!" The slightly raised voice and change in tone indicates urgency, and, in each case, the one word instruction lets your puppy know what it should be doing to get back on track again.

Even for more serious transgressions, harsh punishment is unnecessary. In fact, when you use fun and games, reward-based training methods, banishment is the all-time most effective punishment - a short time-out with no more training game, no more rewards, and no more owner. Calmly and quietly instruct your dog to leave the room, "Rover, Exit!" Banishment need only last for one or two minutes. Then always insist that the dog apologizes and makes up by dutifully coming, sitting, and lying down. When banishment (stopping training) becomes your best punishment, you have achieved the Holy Grail of Dog Training.

Banishment is especially effective if you cheerfully shake the dog's treat jar during the time-out period. When one of my dogs is in a time-out penalty, I make a point of merrily training my other dog and especially giving out lots of "bad-dog-treats." "Good dog, Oso! Why don't you have one of bad-dog-Phoenie's treats?" Works well in our household. On one occasion, I became so irritated that Phoenix was ignoring me that during her time out from the living room I pretended to eat the treats myself. "Mmmmm! Yummy-yummy Phoenie's treats!" When I let her back in the living room, she laid down and wouldn't take her eyes off of me for about half an hour.

Giving the banishment order in a soft and sweet voice and pointing demonstratively to the door will help control your upset and emotions. On the first couple of occasions, you may have to shoo your puppy through the door but it will soon learn to leave promptly following your command. Moreover, after just a few banishments, your soft and sweet "Exit!" command will become a conditioned punishment, having an immediate and dramatic effect on your pup's behavior. At this stage in training, the "Exit!" command becomes an extremely effective warning. Observe your puppy's reaction when you sweetly inquire, "Rover, would you like to pay attention and take heed, or would you prefer to Exit?" Most likely, your pup will wise up immediately. If so, ask it to lie down quietly and let it stay beside you. If not, say "Exit!" in your best sweet and soft voice and demonstratively point to the door.

When banished, most dogs leave reluctantly and remain right outside the door looking in. However, with young puppies with not much training it is better for you to leave promptly when the puppy misbehaves. Therefore, play-train in your pup's long-term confinement area, so that during its time-out your pup does not have the opportunity to get into further mischief. A one-to-two-minute time-out is sufficient, and then return to the puppy's area and ask it to make up and show some respect by coming, sitting, and lying down on request.

Grabitis

Twenty percent of dog bites occur when a family member reaches to grab the dog by the scruff or collar. One doesn't need to be a rocket scientist to figure this out. Obviously, the dog has learned that when people grab it by the collar bad things often happen. Consequently, the dog becomes hand-shy, plays Catch-Me-if-You-Can, or reacts defensively. It is potentially dangerous to have a dog dodge you when you reach for its collar. For example, you need to know you could grab your dog if it tried to dash out the front door.

So, teach your puppy to enjoy being grabbed by the collar. First, prevent your pup from forming negative associations to human hands, and second, teach your pup that being taken by the collar has only positive consequences.

1. If you let your puppy play without interruption, and then take it by the collar to end the play session, of course it will come to dislike your reaching for its collar, since it signals the end of the play session. Starting in the house and later in the park, frequently interrupt puppy play sessions by taking your puppy by the collar, asking it to sit, praising it, offering a piece of kibble, and then letting it go play again. Thus, the puppy learns that being taken by the collar is not necessarily the end of the play session. Instead it is a short time-out for refreshment and a few kind words from its owner before getting back to play again. Also, every time you interrupt the play session, you may use resumption of play to reward your puppy for sitting and allowing you to take it by the collar;

2. If you lead or drag your puppy into confinement, it will no doubt come to dislike being taken by the collar, as it will come to dislike confinement. Instead, teach your puppy to

enjoy confinement. Stuff a bunch of hollow chewtoys with kibble and put them in your puppy's confinement area, and then close the door with your puppy on the outside. In no time at all, your puppy will beg to go inside. Now simply instruct your pup, "Go to your Doggy Den (or Bed, or Crate)" or "Go to your Puppy Playroom (long-term confinement area)," and open the door. Your pup will happily rush inside and settle down peacefully with its chewtoys.

3. Above all, promise your puppy that you will never (NEVER) call your puppy and then grab it by the collar to reprimand or punish. Doing this just once will make it hate coming when called and hate your reaching for its collar. If you punish your puppy after it comes to you, it will take longer to come the next time. Eventually slow recalls will become no recalls. Your puppy will still misbehave; only now, you will be unable to catch it! If you ever punish your puppy after taking its collar, it will soon become hand-shy, evasive, and defensive.

To prevent your puppy from becoming hand-shy, take hold of its collar and then offer a piece of kibble. Repeat this procedure many times throughout the day, and with each successive trial progressively increase the speed with which you reach for the collar. Your puppy will soon develop a strong positive association with being grabbed and may even look forward to being grabbed.

If your puppy is already even a tiny bit hand-shy, the last thing you want to do is reach for its collar. Instead, practice reaching for and handling areas it does not mind having touched or actually enjoys having touched. Then, gradually and progressively work towards the collar. Using kibble as a training treat, start by offering the dog a treat to let it know the game's afoot. "Not a bad start," thinks the dog. Then touch the tip of its tail and immediately offer another treat for its trouble. Trouble? "No trouble," thinks the dog. If it is possible to touch the tip of the tail, then surely it is possible to touch just one inch down from the tip. Give the dog another treat and touch two inches down, then three inches down, and so on. On each repetition, touch the dog a little closer to his collar. It is only a matter of time before you can reach for and handle the dog's collar without upsetting the dog. When touching the dog's collar for the first couple of times, offer one or two pieces of freeze-dried liver.

The key to progressive desensitization is to work slowly. If you even suspect the dog is a little intimidated or uneasy, go right back to square one (in this case, the tip of the tail) and this time work slower.

"J Ate My Dogs Homework!"

*- and other common excuses
for not socializing your puppy -*

"He's fine with me."
Wonderful! Certainly the first step of socialization is to have the puppy perfectly friendly with the family. But it is imperative that the pup become Mr. Sociable with friends, neighbors, visitors, and strangers so that it does not object to being examined by the veterinarian or playfully grabbed and hugged by children.

"We have a big family; our puppy gets more than enough socialization."
Not true! In order to be accepting of strangers as an adult, your puppy needs to meet at least three unfamiliar people each day, not the same people over and over again.

"I don't have any friends to help me socialize my puppy."
Well, you soon will. Socializing your puppy will do wonders for your social life. Invite your neighbors over to meet the pup. Invite people over from work. Check out the puppy classes in your area and invite over some puppy owners from there. They will more than appreciate the problems you are about to encounter in the future.

If you cannot get people to come to your home to meet the puppy, take it to safe places to meet people. Do not put it on the ground in public places that may have been frequented by unvaccinated adult dogs until it is at least three months old and

"I Ate My Dogs Homework!"

current with its vaccinations. Buy a soft carrier and take your puppy on errands, for example, to the bank, the bookstore, or hardware store. See if you can take your puppy to work. Later on, you will be able to take your pup to puppy classes, to dog parks, and on neighborhood walks. But it needs to meet lots of people right away. So whatever you do, do not keep your puppy a secret.

"I don't want my dogs to accept food treats from strangers."
Perhaps your concern is that someone may poison the dog. As a rule, dogs are only poisoned when left alone in backyards (because they are not housetrained and therefore cannot be left safely indoors), or when let loose to range and roam. But you are not inviting dog-hating strangers to interact with your puppy. Instead, you are inviting over selected family, neighbors, and friends. Regardless, every puppy should be taught never to touch or take any object (including food) from any person's hand unless first requested, "(Puppy's name), Take it," or some such command. Having learned these basic manners, your dog will only accept food from people who know its name and who know the appropriate "Take it" command, namely, from family and friends.

"I don't want my dog to like strangers. I want it to protect me."
Oh come on . . . try telling that to your veterinarian, or to your children's friend's parents. However, if you mean you want your dog to perform some protective function, that's a different matter. But surely you are not going to leave it up to a poorly

"I Ate My Dogs Homework!"

socialized dog to make decisions regarding who to protect, who to protect against, and how to protect. Any good protection dog has first been super-socialized to the point of total confidence, and then carefully taught how, when, and who to protect. Training your dog to bark or growl on command is more than a sufficient protective deterrent. Your dog may be taught to vocalize in certain situations, for example, when somebody steps onto your property or touches your car. Alarm barkers are extremely effective deterrents, especially if they do not bark when people simply walk by your house or car. Alternatively, you may teach your dog to vocalize to a command such as "Steady" or "Be Nice." The more you urge, "Be Nice! Be Nice!" the more your dog obediently lunges and barks. An unwelcome person will steer clear thinking that you cannot control your dog.

"I don't have the time."
Then give the puppy to someone who does have the time! This puppy may still be saved, if someone is willing to take the time to socialize it.

"I need to alpha roll and dominate my pup to get it to respect me."
Not necessarily. Or, not at all. If you physically force and dominate your puppy, it won't respect you. It may heed your commands – grudgingly and fearfully - but it certainly won't respect you. More likely, your dog will grow to resent you.

Besides, there are easy and enjoyable ways to get your dog to show respect. Years ago in puppy class, I remember a young

"I Ate My Dog's Homework!"

couple who had a four year old daughter named Kristen and a Rottie named Panzer. In class, Kristen had the dog better trained than her parents and could consistently get Panzer to come, sit, lie down, and rollover. Kristen would give Panzer a tummy rub when he was lying on his side and he would raise his hind leg to expose his belly. Kristen would talk to Panzer in a squeaky little voice. Kristin squeaked and Panzer did it. Or, we could say that Kristen requested and Panzer agreed. Or, that Kristen commanded and Panzer obeyed. More importantly, though, Panzer happily and willingly complied. And when it comes to children training dogs, happy willing compliance is the only kind of compliance that is safe and makes sense.

Was Kristen dominating Panzer? Oh absolutely! But in a much more effective way than by using brute force. As a child, Kristen had to use brain instead of brawn to control Panzer's behavior. Kristen mentally dominated Panzer's will.

Kristen's training engendered Panzer's respect and friendship. Panzer respected her wishes. Also, by approaching promptly off-leash, Panzer demonstrated that he liked Kristen. By sitting and lying down, Panzer showed that he really liked Kristen and wanted to stay close to her. By rolling over, Panzer displayed appeasement. And by lifting his leg to expose his inguinal area, Panzer displayed deference. In doggy language, exposing the inguinal region means, "I am a lowly worm. I respect your higher rank, and I would like to be friends."

If you want your puppy to respect you, lure/reward train it to come, sit, lie down, and rollover. If you want your puppy to

"I Ate My Dog's Homework!"

show deference, teach it to lick your hand or shake hands. Licking and pawing are both active appeasement gestures - signs of wanting to be friends. If you would like your puppy to show doggy deference, tickle its goolies when it is lying on its side and watch it raise its hind leg to expose its inguinal area.

"Dogs of this breed are particularly hard to handle."
Using this excuse to give up on handling, gentling, and socialization exercises is too silly for words. If your research on dog breeds has convinced you that you truly have a difficult breed, you should double or triple the socialization and handling exercises, wind back all developmental deadlines, and start each batch of exercises earlier. Strangely enough, though, I have heard this excuse given for just about every breed of dog. As soon as you think that your chosen breed is too much dog for you, seek help immediately. Find a trainer who can teach you how to handle your puppy before you cause irreparable damage to its temperament.

"My spouse/significant other/parent/child/living companion selected the most dominant pup in the litter."
Did you remember the cardinal rule of puppy selection, that all family members be in complete agreement? Well, it's a bit late for that now, and so I would suggest the same advice as above. As soon as you suspect you have a difficult pup, double or triple the socialization and handling exercises and start each batch of exercises earlier. Additionally, you might consider learning how

"J Ate My Dogs Homework!"

to train your spouse, significant other, parent, child, or living companion.

"Something is genetically wrong with the puppy."
Same advice as above: As soon as you suspect your puppy has some kind of organic problem, double or triple the socialization and handling exercises and start each batch of exercises earlier. It's a bit late for genetical screening, and, in any case, what else can you do - tweak the dog's genes? Many people use breed, dominance, and organic conditions as an excuse to give up on the pup - as an excuse to not socialize and train it. In reality, socialization and training is the puppy's only hope. Your puppy needs socialization and training. Lots of it! Right away!

Regardless of breed and breeding, and regardless of your puppy's socialization and training prior to coming to your home, as of right now any change in your puppy's temperament, behavior, or manners is completely dependent on how you socialize and train it. Work with your puppy and it will get better. Don't work with your puppy and it will get worse. Your puppy's future is entirely in your hands.

"He's just a puppy!", "He's soooo cute!", "He's only playing!", "He'll grow out of it!"
Of course your puppy is only playing − play-barking, play-growling, play-biting, play-fighting, play-protecting a bone, or playing tug-o'-war. If you just laugh at it, your pup will continue playing the aggression game as it grows older, and, in

"*I Ate My Dogs Homework!*"

no time at all, your fully grown adult dog will be playing for real.

Puppy play is all important. Play is essential if a puppy is to learn the social relevance of the vast jumble of behaviors in its doggy repertoire, specifically the appropriateness and inappropriateness of each behavior in each setting. In a sense, play enables a pup to learn what it can get away with. What you need to do is teach your puppy the rules of the game. And the more rules it learns in puppyhood, the safer it will be as an adult dog.

Puppy barking and growling are quite normal and acceptable, just as long as you can stop the noise when you wish. Stopping an eight-week-old puppy from barking or growling is pretty easy. Be still yourself, so the puppy may calm down more easily. Say, "Puppy, Shush!" and waggle a food treat in front of it's nose. Say, "Good dog," and offer the treat when the pup eventually shushes. Similarly, tug-o'-war is a normal and acceptable game, just as long as your pup never initiates the game and at any time, you can get the pup to release the object and sit. Both are easy rules to teach to an eight-week-old puppy. When playing tug-o'-war, instruct your puppy to release the object and sit at least every minute. Periodically stop tugging, say, "Thank you," and waggle a food treat in front of its nose. When the puppy releases the object to sniff the treat, praise it, and ask it to sit. When it sits, praise it profusely, offer the food treat, and then resume the game.

Later sections offer guidelines for the object guarding-game, play-biting, and play-fighting.

Barking and Growling on Cue

A puppy can easily be trained to bark and growl on command and this has many practical uses. Tell it, "Speak!" (or "Steady!") and then have someone ring the doorbell to prompt the pup to bark. After several repetitions, your puppy will bark when you say, "Speak!", in anticipation of the doorbell. Your pup can similarly be taught to growl on command. While playing tug-o'-war, ask your pup to growl and tug vigorously on the toy. When it growls, praise it enthusiastically, say, "Puppy, Shush!", stop tugging, and let it sniff the food treat. When the pup stops growling, praise it calmly, and offer the food treat.

Teaching your puppy to bark and growl on cue facilitates teaching "Shush!" You may practice teaching "Shush!" at your convenience (when you request it to vocalize), rather than

Training a dog to bark and growl on command inspires confidence in both dog and owner. Putting barking and growling on cue facilitates teaching "Shush!"

trying to quieten the pup when it is over-the-top with excitement (when someone is at the front door) or afraid (of an approaching stranger). Alternate "Speak!" and "Shush!" until your pup has it perfect. It will soon learn to shush at times when it is obediently barking or growling. Now your puppy will understand when you ask it to be quiet when it is excited or afraid.

A noisy dog tends to frighten people more than a quiet dog, especially a dog that barks repetitively and works itself into a frenzy. A simple, well-trained "Shush!" request will quickly quiet and calm the dog and make it less scary to visitors and especially to children.

Teaching "Shush!" is only fair to your dog. So many dogs are repeatedly reprimanded and punished for barking and growling simply because no one has taught them to shush on command. The sad thing is that many adult dogs bark only out of excitement, enthusiasm, or boredom. Or they bark and growl as a solicitation to play the same games they played with you when they werepuppies.

Euphemism, Litotes and Other Outrageous Silliness!

"She takes a while to warm to strangers!", "He's not overly fond of children!" and "He's a bit hand-shy!"
How can anyone live with a dog knowing that it is stressed by the presence of strangers and children and scared of human hands? The poor dog must be in a state of extreme anxiety. Just how many times does this dog have to beg, implore, and warn you that it feels uncomfortable around strangers and children and doesn't like people reaching for its collar? This is simply an accident waiting to happen. What if an unfamiliar child should reach for the dog's collar, possibly around the dog's food bowl and the dog is having a bad day and not feeling good? A dog bite for sure. Will we say that the dog bit without warning or reason? The poor dog had at least five good reasons to bite: (1) a stranger, (2) a child, (3) reaching for collar, (4) proximity to its food bowl, and (5) not feeling good. Also, the dog has been warning its family repeatedly for some time.

If there is anything that upsets your puppy, desensitize it to that specific stimulus or scenario immediately. Help your puppy build up its confidence so that it may deal with everyday events without being stressed or scared. The required confidence-building exercises have all been described. Use them!

73

3. *Guarding Valued Objects*

Object-guarding, a common problem with family dogs, will develop throughout puppyhood if owners allow it to. Owners may fail to notice their adolescent dog becoming increasingly possessive and protective. Some may actually encourage their puppy's protective displays, thinking they are cute.

It is natural for dogs to protect their possessions. In the wild, a wolf would hardly pop next door to borrow a cup of bones. Domestic dogs quickly learn that once something is gone, it is gone. So it is not surprising to find dogs trying to keep their possessions away from people.

Bitches are more likely to guard objects than male dogs. In a domestic pack, it is fairly common to see a very low-ranking bitch successfully defend her bone from a relatively high-ranking male dog. In fact, The Bitch's First Amendment to Male Hierarchical Rule is "I have it and you don't!" With male dogs, nothing better advertises insecurity and lack of confidence than object guarding. Object-guarding is common with middle-ranking insecure male dogs. It is definitely not "topdog behavior" at all. In fact, true topdogs are confident in their position and usually quite willing to share a bone, toy, or food bowl with lower-ranking individuals.

If you frequently take food or toys away from your puppy, and it never gets them back, your pup will learn that relinquishing an object likely means it will never see it again. Understandably, your pup might develop behaviors to keep objects away from you. It may run and hide with the object, hold on tight with its jaws, growl, snarl, and maybe snap.

If you find you are backing down when your puppy is protecting any object, and are at a loss for what to do, seek help from a pet dog trainer immediately. This problem will quickly get out of hand, and soon you will have an adult dog backing you down. Retraining adult dogs which are protective of valued objects is complicated, time-consuming, and not without danger. You will definitely require assistance from an experienced trainer or behavior counselor. On the other hand, preventing this in puppyhood is easy and safe.

First make sure that your puppy develops a strong chewtoy habit. If it always wants to play with its chewtoys, it will not

You can easily teach your puppy "Off!" and "Take it" when handfeeding kibble. Say, "Take it," and handfeed a piece of kibble. Repeat this three more times. Then say, "Off!" and present the kibble firmly hidden in your fist. Let the puppy worry at your fist for as long as you like. The puppy will paw and mouth your hand. (Of course, if the puppy's teeth cause pain, yelp! Ignore your puppy for a thirty-second time-out, and then instruct the pup to come, sit, and lie down before proceeding with the exercise.) Eventually, your pup will temporarily give up and withdraw its muzzle. As soon as the pup relinquishes contact with your hand, say "Take it!" and open your hand so that the puppy may take the kibble from your palm. Repeat the sequence over and over, progressively increasing the requisite length of non contact before you instruct your pup to take the kibble each time. I find it helps to praise the puppy for non-contact by counting "good dogs": "Good Dog One, Good Dog Two, Good Dog Three . . . and so on." Once your puppy has learned not to touch your hand for a count of ten "good dogs," you may present the kibble between finger and thumb when instructing "Off!" or Take it!" Eventually, you may practice saying "Off!" and placing the kibble on the floor and then picking it up again before saying, "Take it!"

seek out inappropriate objects which need to be taken away. Additionally, teach your pup to voluntarily relinquish its chewtoys upon request.

Basically, you have to teach your puppy that voluntarily relinquishing an object does not mean losing it for good. Your puppy should learn that giving up bones, toys, and tissues means receiving something better in return - praise and treats - and also later getting back the original object.

Teaching "Off!" has many useful applications

The Token System - Exchanging Valued Commodities for Treats

Start working with objects that both you and your puppy can hold at the same time, such as a rolled newspaper or a Kong on a rope. Physical contact is a very big part of the possession game. Your puppy will be less likely to try to protect an object if you still have hold of it. However, as soon as you let go your pup will be more likely to defend its prize.

As practiced before, tell your puppy "Off!" and then, "Take it!" Waggle the object in front of its muzzle enticingly. Praise your puppy when it takes hold. Do not let go of the object. Say,

"Puppy, Thank you," stop waggling the object to encourage your puppy to stop tugging, and with your other hand, waggle a very tasty treat (freeze-dried liver) in front of its nose. Praise your puppy as soon as it opens its mouth and you have regained full possession of the object. Continue praising as you offer one, two, or three treats (maybe luring the puppy to sit or lie down as you do so). Then instruct your pup to take the object again and repeat the procedure. When your puppy has promptly relinquished the object upon request five times in a row, you may let go of the object each time. Now you are ready to work with smaller objects, such as a Kong without a rope, tennis balls, Biscuit Balls, sterilized bones, or other toys. Once your pup eagerly takes and receives promptly, simply drop or toss the object and say, "Thank you." Voila! Your very own faithful retriever pup!

Retrieving is a lot of fun and good exercise. It has numerous applications, such as looking for lost keys, fetching slippers, and clearing up dog toys. Puppies love retrieving and quickly develop confidence about surrendering objects. Puppies think it's a great deal. They temporarily swap their toys for treats, the owner safely holds the toy while they enjoy the treat, and then they get the toy back to exchange for more treats.

In fact, some puppies enjoy proffering objects so much that it may become a bother to the owner. If your pup offers too many unsolicited presents, simply instruct it, "Take it to your bed." In fact, this is one of the best ways to teach your puppy to clear up its toys.

By teaching your puppy to retrieve objects, wht had intrinsic value as a toy now has additional value as a token which may be exchanged for praise and reward. Playing Fetch with your puppy is a wonderful way to supercharge its toys, increase their effectiveness as lures and rewards for training, and greatly increase the likelihood that a bored puppy will seek out its toys to play with rather than inappropriate household or outdoor articles.

Once the above exercises are working, increase the intrinsic value of the objects by stuffing the Kong or sterilized bone with treats. Before your puppy is ten weeks old, you should have done lots of confidence-building exercises with meaty bones and the food bowl. Even with a ten-week-old puppy, I would advise having an assistant for these exercises. Tie a length of stout string to one end of the meaty bone. Should the pup growl, have your assistant yank on the string to pull the bone away, and quickly cover it with a plastic garbage bucket. The plastic bucket may also be used to cover the pup's food bowl should the pup act up during food bowl exercises.

Don't waste time reprimanding the pup for growling. Instead, make sure to praise and reward your puppy as soon as it stops growling. Additionally, you must make sure that a

A puppy may become protective and defensive if allowed to chew a bone in private and without interruption. Until you are quite comfortable taking bones away from your puppy, never let it have a bone on its own. Instead, say, "Off!" and "Take it!" as before, but hold on to the bone as your puppy chews. Periodically say, "Thank you!" and waggle a very tasty treat in front of the puppy's nose as you withdraw the bone. Hold the bone as the puppy eats the treats and then instruct the pup to sit and lie down before repeating the sequence over and over.

growling puppy immediately loses its bone or food bowl. Many puppies will initially growl when food is removed. These are not bad dogs; they are normal dogs. Growling is quite natural. However, your puppy must learn that growling doesn't work so that this behavior does not escalate and continue into adolescence. As your puppy develops confidence, it will learn that there is no reason to growl because you have no intention of stealing its food. When the puppy stops growling, praise it, back up, and have it sit and lie down, give it back the object, and then repeat the procedure.

If you have problems with object/food guarding exercises, seek help immediately. Do not wait until your puppy is three months old.

The Food Bowl

Many old-time dog training books advise not going near a dog when it is eating. Whereas it may be sound advice to let a trustworthy adult dog eat in peace, this does not mean letting untrained puppies eat alone. If a pup grows up eating alone, it may not want its mealtimes disturbed as an adult. Eventually, someone is bound to bother the dog when it is eating, whereupon it may respond in a characteristically canine, food-protective fashion and growl, snarl, snap, lung, and maybe bite.

By all means, tell people not to bother your dog when it is eating, but first be certain your puppy is totally trustworthy around its food bowl. Teach your puppy not simply to tolerate people around its food bowl, but to thoroughly look forward to dinner-time guests.

Hold your pup's bowl while it eats kibble. Offer tasty treats and handle the puppy, and it will learn its dinners are more enjoyable when people are present, (petting and treats are included). Let the puppy eat kibble from its bowl, offer a tasty treat, and then temporarily remove the bowl as the puppy enjoys the treat. Then try removing the bowl prior to offering a treat. Your pup will soon look forward to your removing the bowl and the kibble, since it signals that a tasty treat is imminent.

As your puppy is eating dry kibble from its bowl, quickly put your hand in the bowl and offer a tasty treat. Give your puppy time to reinvestigate the dry kibble to check for more treats and to recommence eating. Then plunge your hand in the bowl and offer another treat. Repeat the procedure several times. Your pup will soon become accustomed and look forward to sudden hand movements around its food bowl. This exercise impresses puppies to no end - it's like the magician who pulls a flower, an egg, or a dove from behind someone's ear.

Make sure your dogs sit for their supper.

Sit with your puppy while it is eating and have family members and friends walk by. Each time someone approaches, spoon a small dollop of canned food on top of the kibble. Your puppy will quickly make the association between approaching people and juicy canned food being added to its kibble. Later, have family and friends approach and toss a treat into the puppy's bowl. Soon your puppy will welcome the dinnertime presence and presents of people.

The Delinquent Waiter Routine

Have you ever been kept waiting for an hour in a restaurant, eating bread and drinking water and you haven't even ordered? "Where is that waiter? I wish he would hurry over." Well, the delinquent waiter routine prompts the same reaction in puppies. Most will beg you to approach their bowl.

Have your puppy sit while you weigh out its dinner kibble in a bowl on the counter and then put the pup's bowl on the floor. You have to capture your puppy's reaction on camera. It will look at the bowl with disbelief because you put only one piece of kibble in its bowl. Your pup will look back and forth between you and its bowl, gobble down the one piece of kibble, then thoroughly sniff the empty bowl. Casually walk away from the bowl and busy yourself. Maybe inquire as to whether your puppy enjoyed its dinner or not. "Was everything to your liking Ma'am? Are you ready for your second course?" Wait until your puppy begs for more, walk over, pick up its bowl, place in one more piece of kibble, wait for your pup to sit, and then put its bowl on the floor.

Your puppy will become calmer and its manners will improve with each "course." Also, by feeding your puppy's dinner in many small courses, it will welcome your approaches.

Paper Tissue Issues!

Some time a ago, I consulted on a case of a one-year-old dog who stole used Kleenex tissues and irritated its owner by playing Catch-Me-if-You-Can. The dog ran under a bed, the owner poked it with a broomstick, and the dog bit her on the wrist. I have since dealt with many similar cases. For paper-tissue theft to escalate to the point of both owner and dog physically abusing each other is extremely silly. If you don't want your dog to steal paper tissues, dispose of them. On the other hand, if the dog finds paper tissues intriguing, use them as lures and rewards in training, or give the dog one a day as a toy. Regardless, it is essential that you teach your young puppy to exchange rolled newspaper, toilet rolls, or individual paper tissues for food treats, so that it does not becomes possessive and protective of paper products.

"She's a bit tricky around her food bowl."
It is surprising how many owners say this, yet do nothing to resolve the problem. If you ever sense your puppy is even a little bit possessive or protective of any object, do something about it immediately. The requisite confidence-building exercises have all been described. If you think the problem is beyond your control, seek help immediately, while your puppy is still a puppy.

5th DEVELOPMENTAL DEADLINE
By Four and a Half Months of Age

Learning Bite Inhibition

Puppies bite - and thank goodness they do. Puppy biting is a normal, natural, and necessary puppy behavior. Puppy play-biting is the means by which dogs develop bite inhibition and a soft mouth. The more your puppy bites and receives appropriate feedback, the safer its jaws will be in adulthood. It is the puppy which does not mouth and bite as a youngster whose adult bites are more likely to cause serious damage.

The puppy's penchant for biting results in numerous play-bites. Although its needle-sharp teeth make them painful, its weak jaws seldom cause serious harm. The developing puppy should learn that its bites can hurt long before it develops jaws strong enough to inflict injury. The greater the pup's opportunity to play-bite with people, other dogs, and other

83

animals, the better its bite inhibition will be as an adult. For puppies that do not grow up with the benefit of regular interaction with other dogs and other animals, the responsibility of teaching bite-inhibition lies with the owner.

After all the above puppy socialization and handling exercises, your dog will be unlikely to want to bite - because it likes people. However, should your dog snap or bite because it has been frightened or hurt, one hopes that it causes little if any damage because it developed good bite inhibition during puppyhood. Whereas it is difficult to socialize a dog and prepare it for every potentially scary eventuality, it is easy to ensure that as a puppy it develops reliable bite inhibition.

Even when provoked to bite, a dog with well established bite inhibition seldom breaks the skin. As long as a dog's bite causes little or no damage, behavioral rehabilitation is comparatively easy. But when, as an adult, your dog inflicts deep puncture wounds, rehabilitation is much more complicated, time-consuming, and potentially dangerous.

Without a doubt, good bite inhibition is the single most important quality of any companion dog. Moreover, a dog must develop bite inhibition during puppyhood, before it is four and a half months old.

Good Bite-Inhibition

Good bite-inhibition does not mean that your dog will never snap, lunge, nip, or bite. Good bite-inhibition means that should the dog snap and lunge, its teeth will seldom make skin contact; Should the dog's teeth ever make skin contact, the inhibited "bite" will cause little, if any, damage.

Case Histories

No matter how well you try to socialize your dog and teach it to enjoy the company and actions of people, the unforeseen and unpredictable happens. Here are a just a few case histories:

* A friend of the owner unintentionally slammed a car door on a dog's tail;
* A woman wearing high heels unintentionally stepped on her sleeping Rottweiler's leg;
* An owner grabbed his Jack Russell by the collar;
* A groomer was combing out a Wheaten's matted coat.;
* A veterinarian was fixing a Bernese Mountain Dog's dislocated elbow;
* A visitor tripped and flew headlong to butt heads with an Airedale chewing its bone.;
* A three-year-old child (who shall remain nameless) wearing a Superman cape jumped from a coffee table and landed on the ribcage of a sleeping Malamute.

The Rottweiler and Bernese both screamed. The Bernese lay perfectly still and did not attempt to bite. All the other dogs Grrrrwuffffed and quickly turned their muzzles towards the person. The Malamute got up and left the room. Both the Rottweiler and Jack Russell snapped and lunged, but neither made skin contact. The Wheaten took hold of the groomer's arm and squeezed gently. The Airedale nicked the visitor's cheek. All of these dogs were pretty friendly most of the time, but what is crucially important is that they had all developed stellar bite-inhibition in puppyhood. Despite extreme fright and/or pain, bite inhibition instantly clicked in (within 0.04 seconds) to check the bite. Consequently, none of these dogs caused any damage and all were successfully rehabilitated.

The dog with the trapped tail mutilated the person's arm with multiple deep bites. This dog was a breed most people consider to be extremely friendly and had been taken on numerous visits to schools and hospitals. Indeed, the dog was extremely friendly, but it had no bite inhibition. During puppyhood, it did not play with other dogs much, and its puppy biting behavior was infrequent and gentle. Because the dog had never displayed any signs of unfriendliness as an adult, there was no warning that it might bite. And because it had never snapped or bitten before, there was no warning that its bite would be serious. For a dog that is likely to spend a lot of time around people, being well-socialized, but with poor bite inhibition is a dangerous combination.

Some people might feel that a dog is justified to bite in self-defense. But that is not what really happened in any of the above instances. In each case, the dog may have felt he was under attack, but in reality it bit a person who had no intention of hurting it. Whether you agree with this or not, the fact remains that we humans have been socialized not to attack our hair dressers, dentists, doctors, friends, and acquaintances when they unintentionally hurt us. Likewise, it is extremely easy, and essential, to train our dogs not to attack groomers, veterinarians, family, friends, and visitors.

The Bad News and Good News About Dog Bites

It is always upsetting when a dog growls, snaps, nips, or bites. But in the vast majority of bite cases, lack of injury provides reassuring proof that the dog has good bite inhibition. The dog bites due to lack of socialization, but it does not do any damage because it has good bite inhibition.

It is reassuring for owners to know that if ever their dog were provoked and pushed to the limit, it would be strongly inhibited from hurting anyone. For example, if tormented by a child, the dog would only growl and snap and would not even make skin contact.

Customarily, dogs with good bite inhibition may be involved in numerous incidents before their snaps even touch the skin and certainly before their bites break the skin. Thus the owner has numerous warnings and ample time for rehabilitative socialization.

The Good, The Very Good,

The Very Good
Well-Socialized with Good Bite Inhibition

A wonderful dog which loves people and is highly unlikely to bite. Even if hurt or frightened, the dog is more likely to yelp or run away. With extreme provocation, the dog might take hold, but it would be very unusual for the teeth to break the skin.

During puppyhood, this dog enjoyed many opportunities to play-fight with other puppies and dogs and to mouth, play, and train with a wide variety of people.

Even though this is a wonderful dog, remember that socialization and bite inhibition training is a lifelong endeavor. May "bite" anyone, but unlikely to cause any harm.

The Good
Poorly Socialized with Good Bite Inhibition

A dog which is standoffish with strangers. Prone to run away and hide and likely to snap or nip if pursued, crowded, or restrained. Unlikely that the nips would break the skin.

Raised with ample opportunity to mouth and play with other dogs and family members, but did not get the chance to meet many people during puppyhood.

The dog's scared and standoffish behavior provides repeated clear warning that the owner needs to rehabilitate the dog. Good bite inhibition allows the owner the opportunity to socialize the dog safely. Also, the dog's scared behavior provides ample warning for potential victims to stay away. Most likely victims are strangers, especially children and men, and especially people who have to handle and examine the dog, such as, veterinarians and groomers. Unlikely to cause much harm.

The Bad, and The Ugly

The Bad

Poorly Socialized with Bad Bite Inhibition

An apparent canine nightmare. A dog which doesn't like many people, barks and growls frequently, and would lunge and bite, inflicting deep punctures. Usually, initial incidents are comprised of a vocal lunge and a single bite with tearing as the dog pulls its head away in preparation for a hasty retreat.

Most likely the dog was raised in a backyard, kennel, or confined indoors with limited contact with other dogs or people. Puppy play-biting was altogether discouraged.

The dog's saving grace is that it loudly and obviously advertises its lack of socialization, so that few people are silly enough to approach within biting distance. Consequently, incidents involving strangers are rare and involve extreme irresponsibility on the part of the owner. In incidents with strangers, the dog usually makes a hasty retreat after a single bite. Usually, owners are the bite victims, since only they are close enough on a regular basis.

The Ugly

Well Socialized with Bad Bite Inhibition

The real canine nightmare – an extremely dangerous dog! The dog's pleasant outward demeanor camouflages the real underlying problem - poor bite inhibition. Loves people and enjoys their company and unlikely to bite unless provoked. However, should it bite, the punctures are deep and the damage is often extreme.

During puppyhood, this dog enjoyed many opportunities to play and train with a wide variety of people, but the owners probably discouraged mouthing and play-biting. Dog-dog socialization was insufficient and play-fighting was probably not allowed.

Anyone who enjoys socializing and playing with the dog may be bitten, including children, friends, family members, and strangers. Each incident may involve multiple bites since the dog is in no hurry to retreat.

Many people consider a dog a "good dog" until it growls or bites, whereupon it is branded a "bad dog." However, it's not really a case of "good" or "bad" dogs, but rather a case of "good" or "bad" socialization and bite inhibition training. A dog's level of socialization and whether or not it ever growls, snaps, nips, or bites depends on how well it was socialized in puppyhood. The degree of puppyhood socialization depends on the owner. But much more important than whether the dog growls and bites is whether the dog causes injury when it reacts defensively, that is, what level of bite inhibition it acquired in puppyhood. The level of bite inhibition determines whether the dog will simply growl, snap and lunge (not making skin contact), nip (not breaking the skin), or bite and inflict deep punctures. Acquisition of bite inhibition in puppyhood also depends on the owner.

Human Bite Inhibition?

No dog is perfectly behaved, but luckily, most dogs are pretty well-socialized and have pretty good bite inhibition. Most dogs are basically friendly, even though they may occasionally be fearful and wary of some people some of the time. Also, although many dogs have growled, lunged, snapped, or even nipped someone at some time in their lives, very few dogs have ever inflicted any appreciable damage.

Perhaps a human analogy will help illustrate the crucial importance of bite inhibition. Few people can honestly say that they have never had a disagreement, never had an argument, or never laid a hand on someone in anger (especially when considering siblings, spouses, and children). However, very few people have ever hurt another person so badly that they had to be admitted to the hospital. Thus, most people freely admit that they are sometimes disagreeable, argumentative, and prone to physical violence. Even so, very few people have severely injured another person. Dogs are no different. Most dogs have several disagreements and arguments each day. Most dogs have been involved in full-contact fights at some time in their lives. But very, very few dogs have ever severely injured another dog or a person. This is the importance of bite inhibition.

Actually, Dogs Are Less Deadly than People

Sadly, it is true that dogs occasionally mutilate and kill people. On average, each year in the United States twenty people, half of them children, are killed by dogs. Such shocking events almost always make the national news, especially when the victim is a child. But even worse, just last year in the United States, about 2000 children were killed! This had nothing to do with dogs, however. The children were killed by their parents! Moreover, these murders did not make the national news. With over six children murdered each day, child murders are too commonplace to be considered nationally newsworthy.

Bite-Inhibition with Other Dogs

Dog fights offer a wonderful illustration of the effectiveness of solid bite inhibition. When dogs fight, it usually sounds like they are tying to kill each other, and it appears they forcibly bite each other over and over. However, when the dust settles and the dogs are examined, 99 percent of the time there are no puncture wounds whatsoever. Even though the fight was a frenzied flurry of activity and both dogs were extremely worked up, no harm was done because both dogs had exquisitely fine-tuned bite inhibition, acquired during puppyhood. Puppies teach each other bite inhibition when play-fighting, their number one favorite activity.

Unless there are vaccinated adult dogs at home, your puppy must live within a temporary doggy social vacuum and dog-dog socialization must be postponed for a while. Until your puppy has acquired sufficient active immunity, it is too risky to allow it to socialize with dogs of dubious immunization history, or with dogs which have been in contact with the urine and/or feces of dogs potentially infected with parvovirus and other serious puppy diseases. However, as soon as your puppy has developed sufficient immunity to safely venture outdoors (at three months of age, at the earliest), there is considerable urgency to catch up on dog-dog socialization. Enroll your puppy in puppy classes right away and take it for walks and to the local dog park several times a day. You will thank yourself for years to come. There is no greater enjoyment than watching your dog-friendly adult dog enjoy playing with other dogs.

Bite inhibition, however, cannot be put on hold. If there are no other dogs at home for your puppy to play with, you have to teach your puppy bite inhibition until it is old enough to go to puppy classes.

Bite-Inhibition with People

Even if your puppy has a couple of canine buddies at home, you will still need to teach your puppy to inhibit the force and frequency of its bites towards people. Additionally, you must teach your puppy how to react when frightened or hurt by people. It should by all means yelp, but it should not bite and it should never bear down.

Even if your dog is friendly and mouths gently, by five months of age at the very latest, it must be taught never to touch any person's body or clothing with its jaws unless requested. Whereas mouthing is essential for puppies and acceptable from a young adolescent dog, it would be utterly inappropriate for an older adolescent or adult dog to mouth visitors and strangers. It would be absolutely unacceptable for a six-month-old dog to approach a child and take hold of her arm, no matter how gentle, friendly, and playful the dog's intentions. It would frighten the living daylights out of the child, to say nothing of her parents.

Young puppies have frequent and lengthy fights. Most fights are an essential ingredient of normal puppy play, but puppies also have occasional scraps to establish and maintain rank. Frequent play-fighting and occasional rank disputes are essential to fine-tune bite inhibition.

Bite Inhibition Exercises

Please read this section extremely carefully. I shall repeat over and over: Teaching bite inhibition is the most important part of your puppy's entire education.

Certainly puppy biting behavior must eventually be eliminated. We cannot have an adult dog playfully mauling family, friends, and strangers in the manner of a young puppy. However, it is essential that this be done gradually and progressively via a systematic two-step process:
First, to inhibit the force of its bites, and, second, to lessen the frequency of bites.

Ideally, the two phases should be taught in sequence, but with more active puppy biters you may wish to work on both stages at the same time. In either case, you must teach your puppy to bite or mouth gently before puppy biting behavior is eliminated altogether

1. Inhibiting the Force of Bites

The first step is to stop your puppy from hurting people, to teach it to inhibit the force of its play-bites. It is not necessary to reprimand the pup, and certainly physical punishments are not called for. But it is essential to let your puppy know that bites can hurt. A simple "Ouch!" is usually sufficient. When the puppy backs off, take a short time out to "lick your wounds," instruct your pup to come, sit and lie down (to apologize and make up), and then resume playing. If your puppy does not respond to your yelp by easing up or backing off, an effective technique is to call the puppy a "Bully!" and then leave the room and shut the door. Allow the pup a minute or two time-out to reflect on the association between its painful bite and the immediate departure of its favorite human chewtoy, and then return to make up. It is important to show that you still love your puppy, only that its painful bites are objectionable. Have your pup come and sit and then resume playing once more.

It is much better for you to walk away from the pup, than to physically restrain it or remove it to its confinement area at a time when it is biting too hard. So make a habit of playing with your puppy in its long-term confinement area. This technique is remarkably effective with lead-headed dogs, since it is precisely the way puppies learn to inhibit the force of their bites when playing with each other. If one puppy bites another too hard, the bitee yelps and playing is postponed while it licks its wounds. The biter soon learns that hard bites interrupt an otherwise enjoyable play session. It learns to bite more softly once play resumes.

The more times a puppy bites you and receives appropriate feedback, the better its bite inhibition, and the more reliable its jaws will be in adulthood. Appropriate feedback to reduce the force of puppy bites comprises: praising the puppy for gentle mouthing, yelping and having a brief pause from play when the pressure increases, and yelping and having a thirty-second time-out from play following painful bites. After each pause or time-out, remember to instruct your puppy to come, sit, and lie down before resuming play.

The next step is to eliminate bite pressure entirely, even though the "bites" no longer hurt. While your puppy is chewing its human chewtoy, wait for a bite which is harder than the rest and respond as if it really hurt (even though it didn't): "Ouch, you worm! Gennntly! That hurt me, you bully!" Your puppy begins to think, "Good Heavens! These humans are soooooo sensitive, I'll have to be really careful when mouthing their delicate skin." And that's precisely what you want your pup to think: that it needs to be gentle when playing with people.

Your pup should learn not to hurt people well before it is three months old. Ideally, by the time it is four and a half months old, that is, before it develops strong jaws and adult canine teeth, it should no longer be exerting any pressure when mouthing.

2. Decreasing the Incidence of Mouthing

Once your puppy has been taught to mouth gently, it is time to reduce the frequency of mouthing. Your pup must learn that mouthing is OK, but it must stop when requested. Why? Because it is inconvenient to drink a cup of tea or to answer the telephone with fifty pounds of wriggling pup dangling from your wrist. That's why.

It is better to first teach "Off!" using food as both a distraction and a reward. The deal is this: Once I say "Off!", if you don't touch the food treat in my hand for just one second, I'll say "Take it!" and you can have it. Once your pup has mastered this simple task, up the ante to two or three seconds of non contact, and then to five, eight, twelve, twenty, and so on. Count out the seconds and praise the dog with each second:

"Good dog one, good dog two, good dog three," and so forth. If the pup touches the treat before you are ready to give it, simply start the count from zero again. Your pup quickly learns that once you say "Off!" it can not have the treat until it has not touched it, for say eight seconds, so the quickest way to get the treat is not to touch it for the first eight seconds. In addition, regular hand-feeding during this exercise encourages your pup's soft mouth.

Once your pup understands the "Off!" request, use food as a lure and reward to teach it to let go when mouthing. Say, "Off!" and waggle some food as a lure to entice your pup to let go and then praise the pup and give the food as a reward when it does so.

The main point of this exercise is to practice stopping the pup from mouthing, and so each time your puppy obediently ceases and desists, resume playing once more. Stop and start the session many times over. Also, since the puppy wants to mouth, the best reward for stopping mouthing is to allow it to mouth again. When you decide to stop the mouthing session altogether, give your puppy a Kong stuffed with kibble.

If ever your pup refuses to release your hand when requested, say, "Bully!", rapidly extricate your hand from its mouth, and storm out of the room mumbling, "Right; that's done it! You've ruined it! Finished! Over! No more!" and shut the door in its face. Give the pup a couple of minutes on its own and then go back to call it to come and sit and make up before continuing the mouthing game.

By the time your pup is five months old it must have a mouth as soft as a fourteen-year-old working Labrador Retriever: Your puppy should never initiate mouthing unless requested, it should never exert any pressure when mouthing, and it should stop mouthing and calm down immediately upon request by any family member.

Whether or not you allow your adult dog to mouth on request is up to you. For most owners, I recommend that they teach their dog to discontinue mouthing people altogether by the time it is six to eight months old. However, it is essential to continue bite inhibition exercises. Otherwise, your dog's bite will begin to drift and become harder as it grows older. It is important to regularly handfeed your dog and clean its teeth each day, since these exercises involve a human hand in its mouth.

For owners who have good control over their dog, there is no better way to maintain the dog's soft mouth than by play-fighting on a regular basis. However, to prevent your puppy from getting out of control and to fully realize the many benefits of play-fighting, you must play by the rules and . . . you must teach your dog to play by the rules. Play-fighting rules are described in detail in our Behavior Booklet, *Preventing Aggression.*

Play-fighting teaches your puppy to mouth only hands (which are extremely sensitive to pressure), but never clothing.

Establishing bite inhibition is so vitally important that a good ninety percent of puppy play involves biting each other. Perhaps we should learn from our dogs.

Shoelaces, ties, trousers, and hair have no nerves and can not feel. Therefore you cannot provide the necessary feedback when your pup begins to mouth too hard and too close to your skin. The play-fighting game also teaches your dog that it must adhere to rules regarding its jaws, regardless of how worked up it may be. Basically, play-fighting gives you the opportunity to practice controlling your puppy at times when it is excited. It is important to establish such control in a structured setting before real-life situations occur.

Out-of-Control Play Sessions

Some owners, especially adult males, adolescent males, and boys, quickly let play-mouthing sessions get out of control. This is why many dog training texts recommend not indulging in games such as play-fighting or tug-o'-war. The whole point about playing these games is to improve your control. And if you play these games by the rules, you will soon have excellent control over your puppy's mouthing behavior, vocal output, energy level, and activity. But if you do not play by the rules, you will soon have an adult dog that is out-of-control.

I have a simple rule with my dogs: No one is allowed to interact or play with them unless they have demonstrated that they can get them to come, sit, lie down, speak, and shush. This rule applies to everyone, especially family, friends, and visitors, that is, the people most likely to ruin your dog's behavior. For active games, such as tug-o'-war, play-fighting, and a unique version of football, I have an additional rule: No one may play with the dogs unless at any time they can immediately get the dog to stop playing and sit or lie down.

Practice "Off!", "Sit!", and "Settle Down" many times during your puppy's play sessions, and you will soon have an easily controllable adult dog, one that has learned to listen to you no matter how excited and worked up it may be. Do not play with your pup without frequent interruptions. Have short time-outs at least every thirty seconds or so to check that you're in control and can easily and quickly get the puppy to let go, calm down, and settle down. The more you practice, the more control you'll have.

Puppies with Soft Mouths

Many gundog breeds, especially Spaniels (and especially the nice Spaniels), have extremely soft mouths as puppies and therefore receive limited feedback that their jaws can hurt. If a puppy does not frequently mouth, bite, and/or does not occasionally bite hard, this is serious. The puppy must learn its limits. And it can only learn its limits by exceeding them during development and receiving the appropriate feedback. Again, the solution lies with puppy classes and off-leash play sessions with other puppies.

Puppies Which Don't Bite

Shy dogs seldom socialize or play with other dogs or strangers. Hence they do not play-bite, nor do they learn anything about the power of their jaws. The classic case history comprises a dog which didn't mouth or bite much as a pup and never bit anyone as an adult - until an unfamiliar child tripped and fell on the dog while it was gnawing on a bone. Not only did the dog bite, but its first bite left deep puncture wounds because it had developed no bite inhibition. With shy puppies, socialization is of paramount importance and time is of the essence.

Similarly, some Asian breeds have an extremely high degree of fidelity towards their owners, and, consequently, tend to be fairly standoffish with other dogs and/or human strangers. Some restrict their mouthing and biting to members of the family, and some simply do not mouth at all. Hence, they never learn to inhibit the force of their jaws.

Non-biting puppies must be socialized immediately. They must commence play-fighting and play-biting well before they are four and a half months old. Socialization and initiating play are best accomplished by promptly signing up for puppy classes.

A Big Mistake

A common mistake is to punish the pup in an attempt to get it to stop biting. At best, the puppy no longer bites those family members who can effectively punish it but instead directs its biting towards those who have no control, for example, children. What is worse, because the pup does not mouth them, parents are often unaware of the child's plight. Worse still, the puppy may no longer mouth people at all. Hence, it receives no training for inhibiting the force of its bites. All is fine until someone accidentally treads on the dog's foot, or shuts the car door on its tail, whereupon the dog bites and the bite punctures the skin because there has been insufficient bite inhibition.

Speed of Development

The large working dog breeds develop slowly and, as long as they have not developed problems, may delay starting puppy classes until they are four months old (by four and a half months at the latest). However, smaller breeds, especially cattle dogs, develop much faster, and waiting until they are four months old is too late. Cattle dogs, working sheep dogs, toys, and terriers need to be enrolled in puppy classes as soon as is safe and certainly by three and a half months at the latest.

Of course, regardless of the size and speed of development of your puppy, to get the most out of its formal education, enroll in a class when your puppy is three months old and then enroll in a second puppy class when it is four and a half months old.

Puppy School

As soon as your puppy is three months old, there is an urgent need to play catch-up in terms of socialization and confidence building with other dogs. At the very latest, before it is eighteen weeks old, your pup should start puppy training classes.

Four and a half months marks a critical juncture in your dog's development, the point at which it changes from puppy to adolescent, sometimes virtually overnight. You certainly want to be enrolled in class before your pup collides with adolescence. I cannot overemphasize the importance of placing yourself under the guidance and tutelage of a professional pet dog trainer during your dog's difficult transition from puppyhood to adolescence.

Puppy classes allow your pup to develop canine social savvy while playing with other puppies in a nonthreatening and controlled setting. Shy and fearful pups quickly gain confidence in leaps and bounds and bullies learn to tone it down and be gentle.

Puppy play sessions are crucially important. Play is essential for pups to learn canine social etiquette, so that later on as socialized adult dogs they would much rather play than either fight or take flight. If not sufficiently socialized as puppies, dogs generally lack the confidence to have fun and play as adults. Moreover, once they are fearful and/or aggressive as adults, dogs can be difficult to rehabilitate. Luckily, these potentially serious problems with adult dogs are easily prevented in puppyhood, simply by letting puppies play with each other. So give your puppy this opportunity. It's not fair to condemn your dog to a lifetime of social worry and anxiety by denying it the opportunity to play during puppyhood.

This is not to say that a socialized dog will never spook or scrap. A socialized dog may be momentarily startled, but it gets over it quickly. Unsocialized dogs do not. Also, socialized dogs, which have learned to deal with all sizes and sorts of dogs, are better equipped to deal with occasional encounters with unsocialized and/or unfriendly dogs.

Dog-Dog vs. Dog-People Socialization

Training a dog to be people-friendly and especially to enjoy the company of its immediate human family is the second most important item in your puppy's education - much more important than socializing it to other dogs. (The most important item in your puppy's educational curriculum is, of course, bite inhibition.)

Although a few common sense precautions make it possible to live quite happily with a dog which does not get along with other dogs, it can be extremely difficult and even dangerous to live with a dog which does not like people - especially if it doesn't like family members! People-friendliness is a much more important doggy quality than dog-friendliness.

Moreover, it is truly wonderful when a dog is dog-friendly, having had ample opportunity to meet and play with other dogs on walks and in dog parks, few suburban dogs are walked on a regular daily basis. Few suburban dogs are given the opportunity to interact with other dogs. For many dog owners, dog-friendliness is simply not a top priority. On the other hand, for owners who consider dog-friendliness important, in fact a major reason for having a dog, their dogs are presumably walked and/or taken to dog parks regularly and so are likely to grow up to be sociable with other dogs. But even for these dogs, people-friendliness is much more important than dog-friendliness, because every day when walked they are likely to meet many strangers, often children.

Most puppy classes are family-oriented, so your pup will have opportunities to socialize with all sorts of people - men, women, and especially, children. And then there is the training game. It will blow your mind how much your pup learns in just its very first lesson. Dogs learn to come, sit, and lie down when requested, to stand still and rollover for examination, to listen to their owners, and to ignore distractions. Additionally, of course, puppy classes are an absolute blast! You will never forget your pup's first night in class. Puppy classes are an adventure, both for you and for your dog.

Remember, you are attending puppy class so that YOU may learn! And there's still an awful lot to learn. You'll pick up numerous useful tips for resolving behavior problems. You'll learn how to control the rambunctiousness and rumbustiousness which are part and parcel of doggy adolescence. But, most important of all, you'll learn how to control your puppy's biting behavior.

The Number One Reason for Attending Puppy Class is to Provide Your Puppy with the Very Best Opportunity to Fine-Tune its Bite-Inhibition.

By now you're probably pretty fed up with your puppy's mouthing and biting. Either your puppy is still biting you too much and harder than you would like, or it is biting less than is necessary to develop reliable bite inhibition. In either case, puppy play sessions are the solution. Other puppies are the very best teachers. "Bite me too hard and I'm not going to play with you anymore!" Since puppies want to spend all their time play-fighting and play-biting, they end up teaching other puppies bite-inhibition.

Classes of young puppies of about the same age generate high energy and activity levels, pretty much on par with groups of similar-aged children. Each puppy stimulates the others to give chase and play-fight, such that the frequency of bites during puppy play is astronomical. Moreover, each puppy tends to rev up all the others, such that the physical nature of the play and the force of play-bites periodically increase to the point where one puppy predictably bites another too hard and receives the appropriate feedback. A young puppy's skin is extremely sensitive, so pups are likely to provide immediate and convincing feedback when bitten too hard. In fact, a pup is likely to receive better feedback regarding the force of its bites during a single one-hour puppy class than it would all week from its owner at home. Moreover, much of the pup's bite inhibition with other dogs will generalize it to good bite inhibition with people, making the pup easier to train and control at home.

Now, as mentioned above, even well-socialized dogs may have occasional disagreements and squabbles. After all, who doesn't? But just as we have learned how to resolve disagreements, with each other and with our dogs, in a socially acceptable manner without tearing flesh or breaking bones, so can socialized dogs. Although it is unrealistic to expect dogs never to have squabbles and scraps, it is absolutely realistic to expect dogs to settle their differences without mutilating people or other dogs. It all depends on the level of bite inhibition they develop while mouthing other puppies in play. So get your puppy enrolled in puppy class right away. Have it develop a supersoft mouth so that all its woofs are friendly and furry.

Other puppies are the best teachers of bite inhibition. By four months of age, puppy play is almost entirely comprised of chasing and biting each other. Do remember, though, to frequently check that your puppy is not out-of-control. Interrupt your puppy's play every minute or so by taking hold of its collar, calming it down, and maybe instructing it to sit before allowing it to resume play. Remember, you want your puppy to grow up to be sociable and controllable. You do not want your puppy to become an uncontrollable, hyperactive, social loon.

"The vet says our puppy is too young to go to class." Understandably, veterinarians care about the physical health of their patients. Common and serious infectious diseases (such as parvovirus and distemper) are a big concern with young puppies, which require a series of immunizations to produce solid immunity. By three months of age, puppies only have 70-75 percent immunity and so there is justifiable concern that they are still at risk if exposed to infection. This is true. But puppy classrooms are pretty safe places, since only vaccinated puppies are present and the floors are regularly cleaned and sterilized. Besides, your puppy's physical health is only part of the picture. Psychological and behavioral health are equally important.

A puppy's risk of infection depends on its level of immunity and the infectiousness of the environment. A puppy's immunity increases with successive immunizations until it approaches 99 percent immunity at five months of age. Different environments range from relatively safe to extremely hazardous. But no animal is 100 percent immune to disease and no environment is 100 percent safe.

If physical health were the only concern, I would advise that puppies not venture out into potentially infected areas until they are at least five to six months old. However, a puppy's behavior, temperament, bite inhibition, and mental well-being are equally as important as physical health. Each year in the United States, an average of five puppies per veterinary clinic die from parvovirius, whereas several hundred are euthanized because of behavior and temperament problems. Indeed, behavior problems are the dog's most common terminal illness during its first year of life. And just as a developing puppy needs immunizations against infectious diseases, it also requires social and educational "immunizations" to prevent it from developing behavior and temperament problems. For all-around health, a young puppy must receive immunization against disease, but it must also get out and about on walks, to dog parks, and to puppy classes as soon as possible. The older the puppy, the better its immunity. Keep your young puppy as safe as possible, (e.g., at home), but as it gets older it may venture out to less safe areas, such as puppy classes. Once your adolescent dog has maximal immunity, it may more safely frequent hazardous areas such as sidewalks, dog parks, veterinary waiting rooms, and parking lots.

It is a sad fact of life that your puppy is always at risk. For example, dried feces (plus parvovirus) may blow in the wind and end up in your garden or home. Or a family member could step in infected urine and feces and track it through the home. So maintain routine hygiene and leave outdoor shoes outside. The safest place for your young puppy is inside your home or fenced backyard. Keep it there until it is three months old. Before your puppy is three months old, it has household manners to master and many pressing socialization exercises to do in the safety of your home. Other relatively safe places include your car and the homes and fenced yards of family and friends. So it is possible for your pup to begin to safely explore the world at large. Just remember to carry it between house and car.

It is fairly safe for puppies to start classes at three months of age. Indoor puppy classes provide a pretty safe environment, but I would still recommend carrying the pup between car and class. Luckily, the breeds which sometimes have immunity problems (e.g., Rotties and Dobes) are slow developers, and it is fine to delay starting class until they are four months old. I actually prefer bigger, slower-maturing dogs to start class at four months so that adolescent problems can be dealt with while the dog is still in class. Otherwise, if a big dog starts class at three months of age, it will graduate at four and a half months and the owner is still under the misapprehension that they are living with a teddy bear.

I would similarly advise to delay taking your puppy to dog parks or for walks in public places frequented by other dogs (and maybe contaminated with a variety of viruses and other infectious agents) until it is at least four months old. You can always practice leash-walking around your house and yard before performing in public, and you should be inviting people to your house on a regular basis.

Carry Your Puppy

Perhaps even more than sidewalks and dog parks, the waiting room floor and parking lot of the veterinary clinic are the two most hazardous areas for puppies with incomplete immunity. While examination tables are washed and sterilized after every patient, waiting rooms floors are generally disinfected only once a day and parking lots hardly ever. Dogs urinate and defecate in the parking lot and occasionally in the waiting room. Urine may be contaminated with leptosirosis or distemper virus, and feces may be contaminated with parvovirus, coronavirus, or a variety of internal parasites. When in the waiting room, keep your puppy on your lap at all times. Alternatively, leave your puppy in the car and carry it directly to the examination room table when your turn comes.

"Our puppy doesn't need to go to puppy classes; he's great with our other dog at home."

Your puppy may be Mr. Sociable with your other dog, but you're in for a shock when your puppy goes out alone, whether for a walk on the street, to a dog park, or to training class. You will quickly find that your dog is not socialized at all. Instead it will likely run and hide and defensively growl, lunge, and snap. Your puppy may appear to be extremely well-socialized and friendly at home, but it is only socialized and friendly to one dog. Also, it has likely become overdependent on one dog, and when it goes out alone for the first time, it will fall apart, missing the security and company of its best friend and bodyguard, your other dog.

Socialization requires meeting a variety of dogs. To keep a socialized puppy socialized, it needs to meet unfamiliar dogs every day. So walk your puppy and take it to dog parks on a regular basis. And enroll it in puppy classes.

It is wonderful that your puppy gets along with your other dogs at home. However, to learn how to get along with unfamiliar dogs, your puppy needs to meet unfamiliar dogs at puppy class, on walks, and in dog parks.

Right: Using a Kong to lure/reward train a pup to sit at Manhattan Dog Training (Manhattan, NY).

Below: Puppies being trained to periodically sit and calm down during the play session in SIRIUS® Puppy Training classes at Citizen Canine (Oakland, CA).

Looking for a Puppy Class

Hopefully, you will have checked out a variety of classes before you get your puppy and so, you will have a pretty good idea of what you are looking for. But here are a few tips:

Avoid Puppy Classes which advocate the use of any metal collar or any means of physical punishment which frightens, harms, or causes pain to your pup. Push-pull, leash-jerk, grab-and-shake, alpha rollover, and domination techniques are now considered ineffective, besides being adversarial and unpleasant. These out-of-date methods are now, thank goodness, by and large a thing of the past.

Remember, this is your puppy. Its education, safety, and sanity are in your hands. There are so many good puppy schools. Search until you find one.

Look for Puppy Classes where the pups are given ample opportunity to play together off-leash and where pups are frequently trained and settled down during the play session, using toys and treats and fun and games. Off-leash puppy play is vital, but equally as important, the play session must include many short training interludes, so owners may practice controlling their pup when it is worked up and distracted. Look for classes where puppies learn quickly and owners are pleased with their puppies' progress. And above all look for classes where the puppies are having a good time!

You be the judge, and judge wisely. Choosing a suitable puppy class is one of your most important puppy husbandry decisions. To receive a list of puppy training classes in your area call:

The Association of Pet Dog Trainers

1-(800) PET DOGS.

6th DEVELOPMENTAL DEADLINE
By five months and thereafter

The World At Large

By now you're probably quite exhausted by your puppy raising efforts. Hopefully though, you are justifiably proud of your well-mannered, well-behaved, highly socialized dog with dependable bite inhibition. The challenge now is to maintain your dog's stellar qualities.

The prime purpose of puppy husbandry is to produce a friendly, confident, and biddable pup, so that you can face the behavior and training challenges of your dog's adolescence, and your dog can deal with the immense social upheaval that dogs, especially males, face as they navigate adolescence. It is much easier to approach doggy adolescence with an already socialized and well-trained dog. However, maintaining your dog's socialization and training through its adolescence can still be tricky if you don't know what to expect and how to deal with it.

Changes You Can Expect As Your Dog Navigates Adolescence

Behavior is always changing, sometimes for the better, sometimes for the worse. Things will continue to improve if you continue working with your adolescent dog, but they will definitely get worse if you don't. Both behavior and temperament will tend to stabilize (for better or worse) as your dog matures around its second (for small dogs) or third (for large dogs) birthday. But until then, if you don't keep on top of things, there can be precipitous and catastrophic changes in your dog's temperament and manners. Even when your dog reaches maturity, you should always be on the alert for the emergence of unwanted behaviors or traits, which you must quickly nip in the bud before they become hard-to-break habits.

A dog's adolescence is the time when everything starts to fall apart, unless you make a concerted effort to see it through to the stability of adulthood. Your dog's adolescence is a critical time. Ignore your dog's education now and you will soon find yourself living with an ill-mannered, under-socialized, hyperactive animal. Here are some things to watch for.

Household etiquette may deteriorate over time, especially if you start taking your dog's housetraining and other good behavior for granted. But if you taught your pup well in its earlier months, the drift in household etiquette will be slow until your dog reaches its sunset years, when housetraining especially tends to suffer.

Basic manners may take a sharp dive when puppy collides with adolescence. Lure/reward training your puppy was easy: You taught your pup to eagerly come, follow, sit, lie down, stand still, rollover, and look up to you with unwavering attention and respect because you were your pup's sun, moon, and stars. But now your dog is developing adult doggy interests, such as investigating other dog's rear ends, sniffing urine and feces on the grass, rolling in unidentifiable smelly stuff, and chasing squirrels. Your dog's interests may quickly become distractions to training, so that your dog will continue sniffing another dog's rear end rather than come running when called. (What a scary thought: That your dog would prefer another dog's rear end to you!) All of a sudden it won't come, won't sit, won't settle down and stay, but instead jumps-up, pulls on-leash, and becomes hyperactive.

Bite inhibition tends to drift as your dog gets older and develops more powerful jaws. Giving your dog ample opportunity to wrestle with other dogs, regularly handfeeding kibble and treats, and periodically examining and cleaning your dog's teeth are the best exercises to ensure that your adolescent dog maintains its soft mouth.

Socialization often heads downhill during adolescence, sometimes surprisingly precipitously. As they get older, dogs have fewer opportunities to meet unfamiliar people and dogs. Puppy classes and parties are often a thing of the past and most owners have established a set routine by the time their dog is five or six months old. At home, the dog interacts with the same familiar friends and family, and, if walked at all, they are walked on the same route to the same dog park, where they encounter the same old people and the same old dogs. Consequently, many adolescent dogs become progressively desocialized towards unfamiliar people and dogs until eventually they become intolerant of all but a small inner circle of friends.

If your adolescent dog does not get out and about on a regular basis and few unfamiliar people come to the house, its desocialization may be alarmingly rapid. At five months your dog was a social butterfly with nothing but wiggles and wags when greeting people, but by eight months of age it has become defensive and lacking in confidence: it barks and backs off, or it snaps and lunges with hackles raised. A previously friendly adolescent dog might suddenly and without much warning be spooked by a household guest.

Puppy socialization was a prelude to your safe and enjoyable continued socialization of your adolescent dog. However, your adolescent dog must continue meeting unfamiliar people regularly, otherwise it will progressively desocialize. Similarly, successful adolescent socialization makes it possible for you to safely and enjoyably continue to socialize your adult dog. Socialization is an on ongoing process.

Dog-dog socialization also deteriorates during adolescence, often at an alarming rate, especially for very small and very large dogs. First, teaching a dog to get along with every other dog is difficult. Groups of wild canids (wolves, coyotes, jackals, etc.) seldom welcome strangers into their midst, but that's exactly what we expect of canis familiaris. Second, it is

The very best way to keep your socialized puppy socialized is by regular walks and visits to your local dog parks.

The first couple of visits to a dog park can be a little scary for your dog. It is OK for your puppy to hide or seek your reassurance. Immediately pick up your puppy if you are at all concerned for its safety; otherwise, try your best not to unintentionally reinforce needy behavior by soothing or petting your puppy while it is hiding. Instead, try to let other people and dogs coax your pup into the open, and then praise your dog enthusiastically whenever it leaves its hiding place.

unrealistic to expect a dog to be best friends with every dog. Much like people, dogs have special friends, casual acquaintances, and individuals they don't particularly like. Third, it is quite natural for dogs (especially males) to squabble. In fact, it is a rare male dog that has never been involved in a physical altercation at some time in his life. Everything was fine with young pups playing in class and in parks, but with adolescent dogs, the scraps, the arguments, and even the play-fighting seem all too real.

A dog's first adolescent fight often marks the beginning of the end of its socialization with other dogs. This is especially true for very small and very large dogs. Owners of small dogs are understandably concerned about their dog's safety and may be disinclined to allow their dogs to run with the big dogs. Here is where socialization starts to go down hill and the small dog becomes increasingly snappy and scrappy. Similarly, owners of large dogs (especially the working breeds) are understandably concerned that their dogs might hurt smaller dogs. Here too socialization goes downhill and the big dog becomes increasingly snappy and scrappy. Now we're in vicious circle: the less the dog is socialized, the more likely it is to fight and thus be less socialized.

"He fights all the time! He's trying to kill other dogs!"
The fury and noise of a dog fight can be quite scary for onlookers, especially the dogs' owners. In fact, nothing upsets owners more than a dog fight. Consequently, owners must strive to be objective when assessing the seriousness of a dog fight. Otherwise, a single dog fight can put an end to their dogs' socialization. In most cases, a dog fight is highly stereotyped, controlled, and relatively safe. With appropriate feedback from the owner, the prognosis for resolution is good. On the other

hand, irrational and/or emotional feedback, besides being upsetting for the owner, can exacerbate the problem for the dog. It is extremely common for dogs, especially adolescent males, to posture, stare, growl, snarl, snap, and maybe fight. This is not "bad dog" behavior, but rather reflects what dogs normally do. Dogs do not write letters of complaint or call their lawyers. Growling and fighting, however, almost always reflects an underlying lack of confidence, characteristic of male adolescence. Given time and continued socialization, adolescent dogs normally develop confidence and no longer feel the need to continually prove themselves. To have the confidence to continue socializing a dog which has instigated a fight, the owner must convince herself that her "fighting dog" is not dangerous. A dog may be obnoxious and a royal pain, but this does not mean it would hurt another dog. Whereas growling and fighting are normal developmental behaviors, causing harm to other dogs is not.

First, you need to ascertain the severity of the problem. Second, you need to make sure you react appropriately when your dog fights, and give appropriate feedback when it doesn't.

To know whether or not you have a problem, establish your dog's *Bite-Fight Ratio*. To do this you need to answer two questions: (1) how many times has your dog been involved in a fight?; and (2) in how many fights did the other dog have to be taken to the veterinarian?

Zero-to-Ten is a common Bite-Fight Ratio for a one- to two-year-old male dog, that is, ten full-contact fights with opponents taking zero trips to the vet. We do not have a serious problem here. Obviously the dog is not "trying to kill" the other dog, since it hasn't caused any injury in ten fights. The dog would have caused damage if it had meant to. Moreover, on each occasion, the dog adhered to the Marquis of Dogsberry Fighting

Rules by restricting bites to the other dog's scruff, neck, head, and muzzle. Surely, there is no better proof of the effectiveness of bite inhibition than, when in a fighting frenzy, one dog grasps another by the soft part of its throat and yet no damage is done. This is not a dangerous dog; it is merely obnoxious in the inimitable manner of male adolescents. Yes, the dog is a bit of a pain, but it has wonderful bite inhibition (established during puppyhood) and has never injured another dog. Solid evidence of reliable bite inhibition (ten fights with zero bites while adhering to fighting rules) makes it extremely unlikely that this dog will ever harm another dog.

Fights are bad news, but they usually provide good news! As long as your dog never harms another dog, each fight provides additional proof that your dog has reliable bite inhibition! Your dog may lack confidence and social grace, but at least its jaws are safe. It is not a dangerous dog. Consequently, resolution of the problem will be fairly simple. Of course, you still have an obnoxious dog in dire need of retraining, since your dog is annoying other dogs and owners just as much as it annoys you. Call the Association of Pet Dog Trainers at (800) PET DOGS to find a Feisty Fido, or Difficult Dog class.

On the other hand, if your dog has inflicted serious wounds to the limbs and abdomen of its opponents in a number of its fights, then you have a serious problem. This is a dangerous dog, since it has no bite inhibition. Obviously, the dog should be muzzled whenever on public property. The prognosis is poor, treatment will be complicated, time-consuming, potentially dangerous, requiring expert help, and certainly with no guarantee of a positive outcome. No dog problem presents such a marked contrast between prevention and treatment.

An adult fighter with no bite inhibition is the very hardest dog to rehabilitate, but prevention in puppyhood is easy, effortless, and enjoyable: simply enroll your puppy in puppy classes and take it to the park on a regular basis. Do not wait for your adolescent dog to get into a fight to let him know you don't like it. Instead, make a habit of praising and rewarding your puppy every time it greets another dog in a

friendly fashion. I know it may sound a little silly - praising your harmless, wiggly four-month-old male pup and offering a food treat every time it doesn't fight - but it's the best way to prevent fighting from becoming a serious problem.

Canine social greetings normally involve a thorough investigation of each other's private parts. "Reading" a dog's olfactory "business card" is usually a prelude to play. Praise your puppy every time it greets another dog. Do not take your puppy's friendly greetings for granted; its first squabble is probably only months, or weeks, away. If you don't want your dog to get into scraps, you must let it know how pleased you are when it greets other dogs and plays in a friendly fashion.

The Secret to Adolescent Success

Always make a point of praising your dog and offering a couple of treats whenever it eliminates in the right place. Keep a treat container by your dog's toilet area. You need to be there anyway to inspect and pick up your dog's feces (before the stool becomes home and dinner for several hundred baby flies). Remember, you want your dog to want to eliminate in its toilet area and to be highly motivated to do so, even when it develops geriatric incontinence.

Similarly, a stuffed Kong a day will continue to keep the behavior doctor away. Your dog still needs some form of occupational therapy to idle away the time when left at home alone. Nothing will prevent household problems, such as destructive chewing, excessive barking, and hyperactivity, or alleviate boredom, stress, and anxiety as effectively as stuffing your dog's daily diet of kibble into a few Kongs.

For your adolescent dog to continue to be reliably obedient and willingly compliant, you must integrate short training interludes, especially emergency sits and long settle-downs, into walks, play sessions, and your dog's other enjoyable day-to-day activities. Maintaining your dog's manners through adolescence is easy if you know how to, but extremely difficult if you don't. See the sections "Training on Walks" (page 127) and "Lifestyle Training" (page 143).

Should socialization ever fail and your dog snap, lunge and maybe nip, you will be thankful that you had the good sense to take your puppy to classes where it learned reliable bite inhibition. Your dog's defensive actions cause no harm but they warn you that you'd better quickly revamp your dog's socialization program and maintain its bite inhibition exercises before it happens again. Which it will. Continue bite inhibition exercises indefinitely. Occasionally handfeed your dog and examine its muzzle and teeth (and maybe clean them) on a regular basis.

The secret to a well-socialized adult dog is at least one walk a day and a couple of trips a week to the dog park. Try to find different walks and different dog parks, so that your dog meets a variety of different dogs and people. Socialization means training your dog to meet and get along with unfamiliar dogs and people. The only way to accomplish this is for your dog to continue meeting unfamiliar people and dogs on a daily basis. Praise your dog and offer a piece of kibble every time it meets an unfamiliar dog or person.

And don't forget to maintain your own improved social life by inviting your friends over at least once a week - just to keep them still involved in training your dog. Ask them to bring along somebody new to meet your dog.

Host a puppy party and invite your dog's buddies from puppy class and the dog park. To offset some of the scarier aspects of the dog world at large - adult dogs, big dogs, and occasionally unfriendly dogs - make sure your adolescent dog has regular opportunity to socialize and play with its core companions.

The Dog Walk

As soon as it is safe for your puppy to go out, take it on walks - lots of them. There is no better overall socialization exercise and no better overall training exercise. As an added benefit, dog walks are good for the health, good for the heart, and good for the soul. Walk that dog! Tie a pink bow to its collar and see how many smiles you get and how many new friends you make. Doggy socialization is good for your social life.

A walk with your dog is the very best socialization and training exercise. And, it is the very best exercise for you.

Housetraining on Walks

If you do not have a private yard or garden, make sure your dog urinates and defecates before you begin your walk. Thus, the walk becomes a reward for doing the right thing in the right place at the right time. Otherwise, when you terminate an enjoyable walk after your dog has done its duty, you end up punishing it for eliminating. Your dog might then start delaying elimination to prolong its walks.

Put your puppy on-leash, leave the house, and then stand still and let the pup circle and sniff. Give it four or five minutes. If it doesn't perform, go back indoors and try again later. Keep your pup in its short-term confinement area for the interim. If your puppy does go within the allotted time, praise it profusely, reward it with a dog treat, say, "Walkies," and off you go. You'll find a simple "no-feces-no-walk" policy quickly produces a speedy defecator.

There are additional benefits to teaching your dog to eliminate prior to a walk. Clearing up the mess and depositing it in your own trash is much more convenient than a mid-walk clean up. Also, walking an empty dog empty-handed is generally more relaxing than walking a dog and lugging around a bag of dog doo.

Make sure your puppy eliminates in your yard or right outside your front door, BEFORE setting off for a walk. A walk is the very best reward for speedy defecator.

Socializing on Walks

Take a few time-outs on each walk. Do not rush your young dog through the environment. Give your dog ample opportunity to relax and watch the world go by. A stuffed Kong will help it settle down quickly and calmly each time you stop.

Never take your dog's even temperament for granted. The great outdoors can be a scary place, and there will be the occasional surprise to spook your pooch. The best approach is to prevent these problems. Handfeeding your dog its dinner on walks helps it form positive associations towards people, other dogs, and traffic. Offer your dog a piece of kibble every time a car, big truck, or noisy motorcycle goes by. Offer your dog a couple of pieces of kibble every time another dog or person

Stop several times during the walk to settle down and read the newspaper, while your dog practices settling down and watching the world go by.

passes. Praise your dog and offer a treat whenever it greets another dog or person in a friendly fashion. Praise your dog and offer three tasty treats whenever a child approaches. And when a child whizzes by on a skateboard or dirt bike, handfeed it the whole bag of food.

Should someone wish to meet your dog, first show them how to use kibble to lure/reward it to come and sit. Ask the stranger to offer the kibble only after your dog sits to say hello. From the outset, teach your dog to always sit when meeting and greeting people.

Don't be forced to use vegetation or deposit slips from your check book.

Remember

to rubber-band an extra plastic bag to your dog's leash.

Training on Walks

When your dog is five month old, puppyhood is over, and you will begin to realize that the canine weight-pulling record approximates 10,000 pounds. Dogs pull on leash for many reasons. The view is always better for the lead dog. A tight leash provides the dog a "telegraph wire" which communicates the owner's intentions, thus affording the dog the luxury of looking around and otherwise checking out the action. Pulling while on-leash appears to be intrinsically enjoyable for dogs. And, we let them do it. Each second the leash is tight, each pulling moment is hugely reinforced by each step the dog takes, forging ahead to investigate the ever-exciting, ever-changing olfactory environment.

Here are a few dos and don'ts on teaching your dog to walk calmly on-leash:

DO practice leash walking around your house and yard from the very beginning and take your puppy for walks in public as soon as it is old enough.

DON'T wait until your dog reaches adolescence before trying to teach it to walk it on-leash in public, unless you wish to provide amusement for onlookers.

DO alternate short periods (15-30 seconds), when your dog walks by your side, with longer periods (a minute or so), when your dog is allowed to range and sniff at the end of the leash. This motivates your dog to walk by your side, as walking side-by-side is regularly reinforced by permission to range and sniff.

DON'T expect your adolescent (or adult) dog to endlessly heel. It will learn that heeling is mutually exclusive to ranging and sniffing. It won't want to heel and will grow to resent training and the trainer (you) for spoiling its fun.

DO consider training your dog to pull on-leash. Thus, instead of being a problem, pulling on-leash can be the solution, an effective reward to reinforce calmly walking by your side. Alternating slack-leash walking and pulling on-leash is enthusiastically endorsed by my Malamutes. Two paws up! Also, on-command leash-pulling is wonderful for ascending steep hills, pulling sleds, soapbox cars, and skateboards.

DON'T allow your dog to decide when to pull on leash. Employ red-light-green-light training. When your dog tightens the leash, immediately stop, stand still, and wait. Once it slackens the leash, or better yet, once it sits, proceed with the walk.

Red-Light-Green-Light

The good old dog walk has to be one of the dog's biggest rewards, second only to a romp in the park. Many dogs go quite crazy at the prospect of a walk, and, of course, the walk only reinforces its craziness. Moreover, dogs pull on-leash with increasing vigor with every step you take, and of course each step you take reinforces the dog's leash-pulling. Luckily, there's a better way. The walk can reinforce your dog's mannerly behavior.

Before going on a walk, practice leaving the house in a mannerly fashion. Say "Walky, Walky, Walkies!" and waggle the dog's leash in front of its nose. Most dogs will go ballistic. Stand still and wait for your dog to calm down and sit. With its walk stalled before starting, your dog will suspect you want it to do something, but as yet it isn't sure what. It will likely offer many creative suggestions, maybe its entire behavior repertoire. Your dog may frantically bark, beg, jump-up, lie down, rollover, paw you, and circle you. Ignore everything your dog does until it sits. It doesn't matter how long it takes; your dog will sit eventually. When it does, say, "Good dog," and snap on its leash. When you snap on its leash, your dog will likely reactivate. So stand still and wait for it to sit again. When it does, say, "Good Dog," take one step towards the door, stand still, and then wait for it to sit once more. Head towards the door one step at a time and wait for your dog to sit after each step. Have your dog sit before you open the door and have it sit immediately after going through the door. Then come back inside, take off the dog's leash, sit down, and repeat the above procedure.

You'll find that the time it takes for your dog to sit progressively decreases as the exercise proceeds. Also, you'll notice, your dog becomes calmer each time you leave the

129

house. By the third or fourth time you leave, your dog will walk calmly and sit promptly.

Don't prompt your dog to sit. Don't give it any clues. Let your dog work it out for itself. Your dog is learning even when it presents a series of unwanted behaviors. It is learning what you don't want it to do. The longer you wait for your dog to sit, the better it learns which behaviors are unwanted. When your dog sits and receives praise and a reward, it is learning what you want it to do.

Dogs love this game. After playing the game for a very short time, your dog learns which green-light behaviors (e.g., sitting) get you to proceed and which red-light behaviors (everything else) cause you to stand still.

When your dog can leave the house in a mannerly fashion, it is time to go for a real walk. Put your dog's dinner kibble in a bag, for today it will dine on the walk. Hold a piece of kibble in your hand, stand still, and wait for your dog to sit. When it does, say, "Good Dog," and offer the kibble. Then take a giant step forwards, stand still, and wait for your dog to sit again. As soon as you step forward, likely your dog will explode with energy. Stand still and wait. Eventually your dog will sit again. Say, "Good Dog," offer the kibble, and take another giant step forwards. As you repeat this procedure over and over, you'll notice your dog sits progressively quicker each time you stand still. After just a few repetitions your dog will begin to sit immediately each time you stop. Now take two giant steps before your stop. Then try three steps and stop, and then five, eight, ten, twenty, and so on. By now you will have discovered that your dog walks calmly and attentively by your side and sits immediately and automatically each time you stop. You will have taught it all this in just one session, and the only words you said were, "Good Dog."

Avoid Unintentionally Energizing Your Dog

If your dog explodes with energy after you take only one step, just think how you must be fueling it with energy if you continue walking when it is pulling on-leash. Start by taking just one step at a time and then wait for the dog to calm down and sit before proceeding with the next step. Obviously, you can not train your dog in this fashion and get somewhere in a hurry, so take relaxed walks with the specific intention of teaching your dog to walk on-leash.

Sit and Settle Down

Have numerous short training interludes during the walk. Stop for a short training interlude every twenty-five yards or so. For example, each time you stop say, "Sit," and as soon as your dog sits say "Let's Go," and start walking again. Thus, every time you stop, resuming the walk effectively rewards your dog for sitting.

Keep most training interludes shorter than five seconds, so as to reinforce quick sits and/or downs or short sequences of body-position changes, such as, sit-down-sit-stand-down-stand. You may periodically reward your dog with kibble if you like, but this is hardly necessary because resuming the walk is a much better treat for your dog. Occasionally insert longer training interludes to practice having your dog walk by your side for 15-30 seconds at a time or to reinforce two- or three-minute settle-downs. Offer a stuffed Kong for your dog's amusement and read a newspaper for yours.

A stuffed Kong may be used as a lure to teach your dog to sit or lie down, and as a source of doggy entertainment while you enjoy the newspaper.

The above techniques will mold your dog's behavior and mend its manners in a single session. By averaging seventy or so training sessions per mile, a single walk will troubleshoot virtually any training problem. For example, you may experience some difficulty getting your excited dog to pay attention and settle down the first few times you stop, but by the fourth or fifth time, it will be easy. After an enjoyable three-mile walk (with 200 or so training interludes), your dog will be nothing less than brilliant.

The reason why this technique is extraordinarily successful is twofold:

1. Repeated training interludes force you to face your foremost fears and conquer them. The troubleshooting nature of these repetitive, training interludes allows you to solve pressing training problems quickly. For example, your problem is not that your dog does not settle down; it does, but only eventually, only occasionally and only of its own volition. You want your dog to settle-down promptly and reliably upon request. Practice over and over in the above fashion, with many short training interludes during the walk. Your dog will comply quicker and quicker with each trial. Eventually, it will learn to comply immediately.

2. Most owners train their dog only in one or two locations, such as the kitchen and training class. So they end up with a good kitchen-dog and a mannerly class-dog. But the dog still doesn't pay attention on walks and in parks. Presumably, the dog thinks that "Sit" only means sit in the kitchen and in class, because they are the only two places where it has been trained. However, with seventy or so training interludes per mile, every single practice session is in a different setting with different distractions - on

quiet streets and busy sidewalks, leafy trails and open fields, near schools, and in park playgrounds. Thus, your dog learns to heed your instructions and quickly and happily comply no matter where it is, what it is doing, and what is going on. Your dog generalizes the "Sit" command to mean sit everywhere and at any time.

With the above exercises, you will soon have a puppy who will sit quickly and settle down promptly with a single request, no matter how excited or distracted it may be. Moreover, your dog settles down willingly and happily because it knows that being told to lie down is not the end of the world and not even the end of the walk. Your dog will have learned that "Settle Down", for example, is just a relaxing timeout with gentle praise and petting before its exciting life as Walking-Dog resumes.

With your now mannerly dog, you'll find that it is quicker navigating country roads and suburban sidewalks than with your previously hyperactive hound. Now you can follow your intended itinerary without being pulled every which way but loose.

Training in the Car

Don't forget to practice in the car. It's the same technique as on the walk. For a couple of days, read the newspaper in the car, having instructed your dog to settle down with a stuffed Kong. Have a short training interlude every minute or so to practice some body-position changes (sit, down, stand, etc.) or place changes (back seat, front seat, seat belt, crate, etc.). It is much easier to train your dog in the car when you are not driving and the car is stationary. Once your dog promptly responds to each request, repeat the exercises with a friend driving. You'll soon find your dog happily responds to your requests when you are driving.

Make sure you teach your puppy to sit and settle-down, and to speak and shush in your stationary car BEFORE you drive anywhere. (Remember, teaching "Speak" facilitates teaching "Shush.")

Once you have a dog which will settle down anytime, anywhere - in the car and on walks - it's time to get it out and about. Be sure to take a bag of kibble with you. Take your dog everywhere - on errands around town, to the bank, pet store, Granny's, to visit friends, to explore the neighborhood, or maybe just for the ride. It's time for picnics in the park, walks, and more walks. And again, always have kibble on hand to give to your dog whenever dogs or people approach. Also, give kibble to strangers to train your dog how to greet them, that is, to sit for a food reward.

Training in the Dog Park

Letting your dog play in the park can be one of the quickest ways to lose control over your adolescent dog, Allow it to play uninterrupted and you'll quickly lose its attention and have no control over it whatsoever. On the other hand, if you integrate training and play, you'll soon develop reliable, off-leash distance control over your dog.

How to Train Your Dog NOT to Come When Called

Many owners let their dogs off-leash without so much as a "please" or a "sit." Often the dog is excitedly bouncing and barking in anticipation of playing. Thus being let off-leash reinforces their boisterous behavior. They delight in their newfound freedom, running around, sniffing, chasing each other, and playing together like crazy. The owners look on and chat. Eventually, it's time to go. One owner calls her dog, the dog comes running, the owner snaps on the leash, and the play session is over.

This sequence of events is only likely to happen just once or twice, because on subsequent trips to the park the dog understandably will not be quite so keen to come to its owner when called. It doesn't take much for the dog to make the association between coming when called and having an otherwise utterly enjoyable romp in the park abruptly terminated. On future trips to the park, the dog approaches its owner slowly with head down. The owner is now doing a fine job demotivating the dog's recall and is inadvertently training the dog not to come when called.

Indeed, slow recalls quickly become no recalls, as the dog tries to prolong its fun by playing Catch-Me-if-You-Can. The irritated owner now screams for the dog to come, "BAD DOG! Come Here!" And, of course, the dog muses, "I don't think so! In the past I have learned that that nasty tone and volume mean you're not too happy. I think it would be a mite foolish for me to approach you right now. You're not in the best frame of mind to praise and reward me appropriately." But you are not going to do this with your dog, are you?

How to Train Your Dog to Come When Called

Instead, you are going to take your dog's dinner kibble to the park, call your dog every minute or so throughout its play session, have it sit for a couple of pieces of kibble, and then let it go play again. Your dog will soon learn that coming when called is an enjoyable time-out, a little refreshment, a kind word, and a hug from you, before it resumes play. Your dog becomes confident that coming when called does not signal the end of the play session. Your dog's enthusiastic recalls will be the talk of the town! When it is time to end the off-leash play session, I like to soften the blow by telling my dogs, "Let's go and find your Kongs!" Before going to the park, I always leave stuffed Kongs in the car and back home as a special treat.

In addition, you might consider teaching your dog an emergency sit or down, which is often better than an emergency recall. Teaching a reliable sit or down is much easier than maintaining a reliable recall. With a quick sit you instantly control your dog's behavior and limit its movement. Once your dog is sitting, you have several options: (1) You may let the dog resume playing; (Either you were just practicing the emergency sit, or the danger has passed.) (2) You may call your dog to you. (The surroundings are changing and it would be safer if your dog were closer; other dogs, people, or especially children are approaching.) Your dog is more likely to come when called if it is already sitting and looking at you, that is, if it is already demonstrating willing compliance. (3) You may instruct your dog to lie down and stay. (The setting is likely to be unstable for a while and it would be safer if your dog were not running around or running towards you. For example, a group of schoolchildren may be passing between you and your distant dog. To call your dog now would scatter the children like tenpins.) (4) Walk up to your dog and put it on leash. For added stability, it is good practice to hold your dog's attention with your hand in a policeman stop signal and continually praise your dog for staying as you approach. (Danger is imminent and a recall or distant stay would be unwise. For example, a herd of one hundred goats is being driven towards your dog. This once happened to my Malamute in Tilden Park.)

Four Steps to an Emergency Distant Sit

The secret to off-leash control is to thoroughly integrate fun training into all of your dog's off-leash activities. Total integration of training and play should be your aim from the very start. Interrupt your dog's off-leash activities every minute or so. Every time you interrupt an enjoyable activity by instructing your dog to sit, for example, and then allow it resume the activity, you are reinforcing the dog's prompt sit with a powerful reward. The more you interrupt your dog's play, the more you may reward it for siting promptly.

First practice the following exercises in safe (enclosed) areas. This can be when your puppy is off-leash in your house or yard, when it is playing in puppy classes, during puppy parties, or when off-leash in dog parks.

1. Every minute or so, run up to your puppy and take it by the collar. Praise the pup, offer a tasty food treat, and then tell it to go play again. At first try this in a fairly small area, e.g., your kitchen with no other distractions. Then try it with just one other puppy present. If you have

difficulty catching your pup, have the other owner grab hers at the same time. Then try with a couple of other puppies present. Gradually increase the number of puppies and size of the area until your puppy is easy to catch when playing, for example, in your fenced yard. Use freeze-dried liver treats during this first exercise so your pup quickly comes to love having its collar grabbed.

2. Once your puppy is easy to catch, dry kibble will suffice. Now, instruct your puppy to sit each time after you take it by the collar. Use the food to lure the puppy into a sitting position, praise the pup as soon as it sits, offer the piece of kibble as a reward, and then tell it to go play.

3. By now your puppy should feel completely at ease with your running up to reach for its collar. In fact, it probably looks forward to it, knowing it will receive a food reward before resuming play. You may find your puppy sits in anticipation of the food reward. This is good, because the next step is to instruct your puppy to sit before you reach for its collar. Run up to your puppy and waggle a piece of kibble under its nose, and once the puppy homes in on the food, use it as a lure to entice it to sit. Praise your puppy as soon as it sits, offer the kibble as a reward, and tell the puppy to go play.

It is vital that you do not touch the puppy before it sits. Some owners are impatient and physically sit the dog down. If you have to rely on physical contact to get your dog to sit, you'll never have reliable off-leash control. If you are experiencing difficulties, go back to using freeze-dried liver.

4. Now that your puppy sits promptly as you approach, you can teach it to sit from a distance. Again try this exercise around the house without distractions before trying it

with other puppies present. Sit in a chair and without moving a muscle, calmly and quietly say, "Puppy Sit," wait a second, then rush towards the puppy saying, "Sit! Sit! Sit!", in an urgent tone but without shouting. Praise your puppy the moment it sits, take it by the collar, offer the piece of kibble as a reward, and then let it resume playing. As you repeat this over and over again, you'll discover that fewer and fewer repetitions of the instruction to sit are necessary before your puppy complies. Also, with repeated trials your puppy sits sooner and sooner and with you farther and farther away. Eventually your dog will sit promptly at a single softly spoken request from a distance.

From now on, whenever your dog is off-leash, repeatedly and frequently interrupt its activity with numerous short training interludes. Ninety percent of the training interludes should be as short as one second. Tell your dog to "Sit" and then immediately say, "Go play." Your dog's quick sit is proof that you have control, and so you needn't push it. You needn't prolong the sit stay. Instead, quickly tell your dog to go play so as to reinforce the quick sit. In one out of ten training interludes practice something a little different. Once your dog sits, instruct it to sit-stay or to down-stay. Or walk up to your dog and take it by the collar before telling it to resume playing.

Integrate Training and Games

Integrate training into doggy games. Playing games with lots of rules is a fun way to train your dog and exercise its mind. Your puppy will learn that games have rules and that rules are fun. Training becoms a game, and games become training.

Above: Three visiting Rocky Mountain Search and Rescue shepherds challenge Oso to a home game of cookie-search in the living room.

Ivan could search and rescue shoes from any hiding place.

Ivan and Oliver were taught to play a complicated game of tug-o'-war with a rope hanging from the buckeye tree at the bottom of the garden. If you don't teach your dogs how to play games, they will make up their own doggy games with their own doggy rules.

A famous author's dogs enjoy their own version of Keepaway Kong on the Couch while their owner researches a book about dogs who never lie.

Integrate Training and Lifestyle

In order to get your puppy to respond here, there, and everywhere, it needs be trained here, there, and everywhere. Train your puppy little but often, at least fifty training sessions a day, with only one or two being more than a few seconds long. The secret is to totally integrate training into your puppy's lifestyle, and into your lifestyle.

Your Puppys Lifestyle

Integrate short training interludes (quick sits and releases) into your puppy's walks and off-leash play. Each quick sit is immediately reinforced by allowing the dog to resume walking or playing - the very best rewards in domestic dogdom. Integrate short training interludes into every enjoyable doggy activity - riding in the car, watching you fix their dinner, lying on the couch, and playing doggy games. For example, have your dog sit before you throw a tennis ball and before you take it back. Progressively increase the length of sit-stay with each repetition.

Similarly, insert short training preludes before all your puppy's enjoyable activities. For example, ask the pup to lie down and rollover for a tummy rub, or to lie down and stay a while before being invited for a snuggle on the couch. Have it sit before you put in on leash, before you open the door, before you tell it to jump in the car, before you allow it to get out of the car, and before you let it off-leash. And be sure to have it sit for its supper.

With total integration, your puppy will see no difference between playing and training. Fun times will have structure, and training will be fun!

Integrate Training into Your Own Lifestyle.

Train on a regular basis and you'll discover that integrated training is easy and enjoyable. For example, call your puppy for a body-position sequence with variable length stays in each position every time you open the fridge, make a cup of tea, turn a page of the newspaper, or send an e-mail. If you instruct the pup to perform a simple body-position sequence on every such occasion, you will easily be able to train your puppy over fifty times a day without deviating from your normal lifestyle. Remember that you are responsible for a young, impressionable, developing canine brain. Exercise that doggy brain. Allow your pup to achieve and enjoy its full potential.

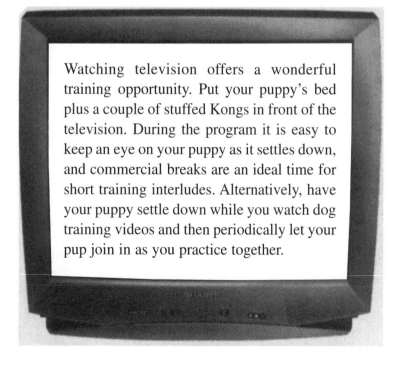

Watching television offers a wonderful training opportunity. Put your puppy's bed plus a couple of stuffed Kongs in front of the television. During the program it is easy to keep an eye on your puppy as it settles down, and commercial breaks are an ideal time for short training interludes. Alternatively, have your puppy settle down while you watch dog training videos and then periodically let your pup join in as you practice together.

Oso practicing sit-stay in the hammock prior to moving on to the settle-down exercise.

Once your dog is well-trained, it may enjoy full run of your house, will be welcome almost anywhere, and may eventually graduate to couch work. My dogs spend most of the time snuggled on the couch. They like the Discovery channel. Occasionally during breaks, I may ask them to do something, like move over, fetch the paper, change the channel, vacuum the living room, or fix dinner. They're highly trained dogs.

Phoenix was always a natural at couch work.

Homework Schedules

All behavior, training, and temperament problems are easy to prevent in puppyhood. The same problems can be time-consuming and extremely difficult to resolve in adulthood. Separation anxiety, fearfulness, and aggression towards people *must* be prevented before your puppy is three months old. Consequently, have family members and friends check that you do your homework each day. Your puppy can't learn if you don't teach it.

Check each box or include a score (number of times, length of time, percentage) where appropriate. Photocopy the homework schedule for each week, until your puppy survives adolescence.

Home Alone in the Household

During its first week in your home, your puppy must learn housetraining, household manners, and how to amuse itself when left by itself. Success depends on (1) your puppy spending most of its time in a self-teaching environment (short-term and long-term confinement); and (2) your puppy receiving all of its food from stuffed chewtoys or being handfed from people (vs. food quickly gobbled down "for free" from a bowl).

Percentage of time your puppy spends in:

	S	S	M	T	W	T	F
Short-term confinement with stuffed chewtoys	❏	❏	❏	❏	❏	❏	❏
Long-term confinement with stuffed chewtoys and a toilet	❏	❏	❏	❏	❏	❏	❏
Playing & training with people with 100% supervision and feedback	❏	❏	❏	❏	❏	❏	❏
Investigating the house with 100% supervision and feedback	❏	❏	❏	❏	❏	❏	❏
Investigating the house or yard with no supervision	❏	❏	❏	❏	❏	❏	❏

With unsupervised free-range access to your house, your puppy will develop a predictable series of problems: housesoiling, chewing, barking, digging, escaping, and other anxiety-induced problems.

Percentage of your pup's daily diet
(kibble and treats) that it received in:

	S	S	M	T	W	T	F
Hollow chewtoys	❑	❑	❑	❑	❑	❑	❑
Handfed as rewards by strangers	❑	❑	❑	❑	❑	❑	❑
Handfed as rewards by family & friends	❑	❑	❑	❑	❑	❑	❑

Number of times you practiced:

Long-term confinement when at home	❑	❑	❑	❑	❑	❑	❑
Short-term confinement in different rooms	❑	❑	❑	❑	❑	❑	❑

Occasionally, put your puppy in its long-term confinement area when you are home to monitor its behavior. As soon as your puppy has leaned to settle-down quickly and quietly with a chewtoy, you will be able to dispense with the crate for short-term confinement.

Number of food rewards that your puppy
received for using its toilet area .... ❑ ❑ ❑ ❑ ❑ ❑ ❑

This is the quickest way to housetrain your puppy

Number of times your puppy
ate from its food bowl .... ❑ ❑ ❑ ❑ ❑ ❑ ❑

Unless you are practicing food bowl exercises (see page 79), you are wasting precious kibble for stuffing chewtoys and for family, friends, and strangers to use as rewards when training the puppy.

Number of chewing mistakes .... ❑ ❑ ❑ ❑ ❑ ❑ ❑

Number of housesoiling mishaps .... ❑ ❑ ❑ ❑ ❑ ❑ ❑

During your puppy's first few weeks at home, any mistake should be viewed seriously. Puppies with housesoiling and chewing problems are usually relegated and confined to the yard where they bark, dig, and escape out of boredom and anxiety. Early confinement with stuffed chewtoys teaches your puppy *what* to chew, *when* and *where* to eliminate, and to settle-down quietly. Keeping your well-behaved puppy indoors prevents it from digging or escaping.

Bite Inhibition

	S	S	M	T	W	T	F
Number of play-mouthing and play-fighting sessions	☐	☐	☐	☐	☐	☐	☐

The more you provide appropriate feedback to your puppy when it mouths and bites your hands, the quicker it will learn to decrease the force of its bites, and the safer its jaws will be in adulthood. The number of times your puppy bites/mouths you will increase steadily as your pup's stamina and desire to play increase throughout puppyhood and adolescence. However, the number of times your puppy hurts you should peak at three and a half months of age as its jaws become more powerful and then decrease as your puppy learns to be more gentle.

Number of times your puppy's biting behaviour hurt you	☐	☐	☐	☐	☐	☐	☐

Daily ouches should have decreased significantly by four months of age. If not, seek help from a trainer immediately.

Number of training interludes (sits or settle downs) per session	☐	☐	☐	☐	☐	☐	☐

You can not interrupt play sessions too many times. Each time you stop playing, resuming play may be used as a reward for stopping.

Number of times you supervised your puppy's play with squeaky toys and soft toys	☐	☐	☐	☐	☐	☐	☐

The above exercise is essential for toy survival and one of the best ways to teach your puppy to be gentle with its jaws. Remember, stuffed animals and squeaky toys are not chewtoys: Their destruction and consumption is extremely dangerous for your dog!

Have you taught your puppy to speak (bark and growl) on cue? Now is the best time to do it.

And, have you signed up for puppy class yet? Puppy classes offer the best controlled venue for your puppy to learn bite inhibition.

Socialization & Training at Home

Your puppy must socialize with at least 100 people before it is three months old. That's just 25 people a week, or four a day. List the number of people who met your puppy:

	S	S	M	T	W	T	F
Total number of people	☐	☐	☐	☐	☐	☐	☐
Number of men	☐	☐	☐	☐	☐	☐	☐
Number of strangers	☐	☐	☐	☐	☐	☐	☐
Total number of children	☐	☐	☐	☐	☐	☐	☐
Number of babies (0-2 years old)	☐	☐	☐	☐	☐	☐	☐
Number of toddlers (2-4 years old)	☐	☐	☐	☐	☐	☐	☐
Number of children (4-12 years old)	☐	☐	☐	☐	☐	☐	☐
Number of teenagers (13-19 years old)	☐	☐	☐	☐	☐	☐	☐

Supervise puppy and human youngsters at all times. Let the puppy sniff the baby's diapers. Protect the baby's face and hands. Toddlers may handfeed and train the puppy if you enclose their hand in yours. Children and teenagers are the very best puppy trainers with instruction and supervision.

Number of Puppy Parties	☐	☐	☐	☐	☐	☐	☐
Number of people at each party	☐	☐	☐	☐	☐	☐	☐
Number of guests who trained your puppy to come, sit, lie down, and stay	☐	☐	☐	☐	☐	☐	☐
Number of funny people at each party	☐	☐	☐	☐	☐	☐	☐

Your puppy needs to be exposed to people wearing hats, helmets, sunglasses, and beards, as well as people acting weird, making funny faces, staring, walking like John Cleese, laughing, giggling, crying, talking loudly, and pretending to argue.

Number of guests who held (hugged/restrained) your puppy	☐	☐	☐	☐	☐	☐	☐

Number of guests who offered kibble
after examining your puppy's: S S M T W T F

Muzzle .... ❑ ❑ ❑ ❑ ❑ ❑ ❑

Two ears .... ❑ ❑ ❑ ❑ ❑ ❑ ❑

Four paws .... ❑ ❑ ❑ ❑ ❑ ❑ ❑

Rear end .... ❑ ❑ ❑ ❑ ❑ ❑ ❑

Number of times a family member
offered kibble after:

Examining the puppy's muzzle .... ❑ ❑ ❑ ❑ ❑ ❑ ❑

Examining both ears .... ❑ ❑ ❑ ❑ ❑ ❑ ❑

Examining each paw .... ❑ ❑ ❑ ❑ ❑ ❑ ❑

Hugging/restraining the puppy .... ❑ ❑ ❑ ❑ ❑ ❑ ❑

Giving the puppy a tummy rub .... ❑ ❑ ❑ ❑ ❑ ❑ ❑

Taking hold of the puppy's collar .... ❑ ❑ ❑ ❑ ❑ ❑ ❑

Grooming the puppy .... ❑ ❑ ❑ ❑ ❑ ❑ ❑

Examining and cleaning puppy's teeth ...... ❑ ❑ ❑ ❑ ❑ ❑ ❑

Clipping puppy's nails .... ❑ ❑ ❑ ❑ ❑ ❑ ❑

Number of pieces of kibble handfed when
teaching the puppy to come, sit, lie down,
and stay .... ❑ ❑ ❑ ❑ ❑ ❑ ❑

Number of pieces of kibble handfed when
teaching the puppy, "Off!", "Take it!",
and "Gennnntly!" .... ❑ ❑ ❑ ❑ ❑ ❑ ❑

Number of toy exchanges (balls, bones,
chewtoys, paper tissue) for kibble when
teaching the puppy, "Off!", "Take it!"
and "Thank you!" .... ❑ ❑ ❑ ❑ ❑ ❑ ❑

Number of food bowl exercises .... ❑ ❑ ❑ ❑ ❑ ❑ ❑

Socialization and Training in the World At Large

The big wide world can be a scary place for a three-month-old pup. Do not rush your puppy through the environment. Chose a quiet street near your house/apartment and, give your puppy all the time in the world to watch the world go by. Make sure you take your puppy's dinner kibble in a picnic bag. After a half-dozen or so picnics, your puppy will be unflappable - been there, done that, like that!

*Handfeed your puppy a piece of kibble each time a person or another dog passes by.

*Offer a liver treat each time a child, truck, motorbike, bicycle or skateboarder whizzes by. Have liver treats for strangers and children to feed to your pup when it sits. Have Puppy Party guests initially expose your puppy to bicycles, skateboards, and over moving blects. This way, the potentially scary stimuli are much more controllable.

*Repeat the above procedure *on a busier street, *in a downtown commercial area, *near a childrens' playground, *in a shopping center, and *in a rural area around other animals. Make sure your puppy gets to spend time exploring *office buildings, *staircases, *elevators, and *slippery floors.

	S	S	M	T	W	T	F
Number of unfamiliar people who met your puppy	❏	❏	❏	❏	❏	❏	❏
Number of unfamiliar dogs who met your puppy	❏	❏	❏	❏	❏	❏	❏

To remain sociable and friendly, your puppy needs to meet at least three unfamiliar people and three unfamiliar dogs each day. Otherwise, it will desocialize dramatically during adolescence (between four and a half months and two years of age).

Number of walks	❏	❏	❏	❏	❏	❏	❏
Number of trips to the dog park	❏	❏	❏	❏	❏	❏	❏

Number of training interludes   S   S   M   T   W   T   F
(sits and downs) per walk .... ❏ ❏ ❏ ❏ ❏ ❏ ❏

Number of one minute settle-downs
per walk .... ❏ ❏ ❏ ❏ ❏ ❏ ❏

Number of recalls or emergency
sits and downs in dog park .... ❏ ❏ ❏ ❏ ❏ ❏ ❏

Number of times your puppy
peed 'n pooped prior to a walk .... ❏ ❏ ❏ ❏ ❏ ❏ ❏

Number of times you trained your puppy
in the car .... ❏ ❏ ❏ ❏ ❏ ❏ ❏

Number of times you praised and rewarded
your puppy after it greeted another dog .... ❏ ❏ ❏ ❏ ❏ ❏ ❏

List your puppy's top ten favorite activities and games that you use as life rewards to integrate training into your puppy's lifestyle.

1. ....   6. ....
2. ....   7. ....
3. ....   8. ....
4. ....   9. ....
5. ....   10. ....

List the games you play with your puppy to make training easy and enjoyable. Check out the list of fun books and videos on page 156.

....
....
....

Number of times you were upset
with your puppy's behavior .... ❏ ❏ ❏ ❏ ❏ ❏ ❏

Number of times you reprimanded
or punished your puppy .... ❏ ❏ ❏ ❏ ❏ ❏ ❏

If things are not going as planned and you are dissatisfied with your puppy's progress, seek help from a trainer immediately.

If you have dutifully accomplished everything described in this booklet, congratulations! You should now enjoy a long life with your good-natured, well-mannered canine companion. Give your dog a special bone today. "Good Dog!" And give yourself a resounding pat on the back . "Well Done! Gooooood owner!"

Shopping List

Many training books, pet stores, and dog catalogs display an awesome and confusing array of doggy products and training equipment. Consequently, I have listed a number of essentials with personal preferences in parentheses.

1. Dog crate (Vari Kennel) and maybe an exercise pen
2. At least six chewtoys - to stuff with kibble and treats (Kong products and bones)
3. Doggy toilet (construct your own)
4. Water bowl
5. Dog food (kibble) - during its first few weeks at home, make sure your puppy receives all food stuffed in chewtoys, or handfed as rewards for socialization, behavior modification, and teaching basic manners
6. Freeze dried liver - for men, strangers and children to win your puppy's confidence (Benny Bully's Liver Treats)
7. Martingale collar and leash (Premier Pet Products)

Most of the above items plus the books and videos (see pages 154-157) are available from your local pet store (where you picked up this booklet), or mail order and on-line from Best Dog Stuff at:
1-(800) 297 0225 or www.besdogstuff.com

Books & Videos

Most book shops and pet stores offer a bewildering choice of dog books and videos. Consequently a number of dog training associations have voted on what they consider to be the most useful for prospective puppy owners. I have included the lists as voted by the Dog Friendly Dog Trainers Group. (Also included in parentheses are the ranks of each book and video as voted by the Association of Pet Dog Trainers - the largest association of professional pet dog trainers worldwide, and by the Canadian Assocaiton of Professional Pet Dog Trainers).

Most of the books and videos are practical puppy raising guides, primarily comprising useful training tips and techniques. In addition I have included lists of my own: A list for those of you who especially want to have fun with your dog, and lists for those of you who are interested in a better understanding of dog behavior and psychology.

TOP FIVE BEST VIDEOS

#1 Sirius Puppy Training - Ian Dunbar
James & Kenneth Publishers, 1987. (CAPPDT #1, APDT #1)

#2 Training Dogs with Dunbar - Ian Dunbar
James & Kenneth Publishers, 1996. (CAPPDT #2, APDT #4)

#3 Training the Companion Dog (4 videos) - Ian Dunbar
James & Kenneth Publishers, 1992. (APDT #2, Winner of the
Dog Writers Association *Maxwell Award* for Best Dog Training Video)

#4 Dog Training for Children - Ian Dunbar
James & Kenneth Publishers, 1996.

#5 Puppy Love: Raise Your Dog the Clicker Way - Karen
Pryor & Carolyn Clark. Sunshine Books, 1999.

TOP TEN BEST BOOKS

#1 How to Teach a New Dog Old Tricks - Ian Dunbar
James & Kenneth Publishers, 1991. (APDT #1, CAPPDT #4)

#2 The Culture Clash - Jean Donaldson
James & Kenneth Publishers, 1996. (APDT #2, CAPPDT #1, Winner
of the DWAA *Maxwell Award* for Best Dog Training Book)

#3 Doctor Dunbar's Good Little Dog Book - Ian Dunbar
James & Kenneth Publishers, 1992. (APDT #5, CAPPDT #6)

#4 Train Your Dog the Lazy Way - Andrea Arden
Alpha Books, 1999.

#5 Labrador Retrievers for Dummies - Joel Walton & Eve
Adamson. IDG Books Worldwide, 1999.

#6 The Perfect Puppy - Gwen Bailey
Hamlyn, 1995. (APDT #8)

#7 Dog Friendly Dog Training - Andrea Arden
IDG Books Worldwide, 2000.

#8 Behavior Booklets (9 booklets) - Ian Dunbar
James & Kenneth Publishers, 1985. (APDT #9)

#9 Puppy Primer - Brenda Scidmore & Patricia McConnell
Dog's Best Friend, 1996.

#10 "Pawsitive" Dog Training - Allan Bauman
Goldenbrook Kennels, 1995.

BOOKS/VIDEOS FOR DOGGY INTEREST

#1 The Culture Clash - Jean Donaldson
James & Kenneth Publishers, 1996. (CAPPDT #1, APDT #2)

#2 Don't Shoot the Dog - Karen Pryor
Bantam Books, 1985. (CAPPDT #2, APDT #7)

#3 Dog Language - Roger Abrantes
Wakan Tanka Publishers, 1997.

#4 Dog Behavior: Why Dogs Do What They Do - Ian Dunbar
TFH Publications, 1979. (CAPPDT #6)

#5 Behavior Problems in Dogs - William Campbell
Behavior Rx Systems, 1999. (CAPPDT #6)

#6 Biting & Fighting (2 videos) - Ian Dunbar
James & Kenneth Publishers, 1994.

#7 Excel-erated Learning: Explaining How Dogs Learn and How Best to Teach Them - Pamela Reid
James & Kenneth Publishers, 1996.

#8 How Dogs Learn - Mary Burch & Jon Bailey
Howell Book House, 1999.

#9 Dogs - Raymond and Lorna Coppinger
Scribner, 2001.

#10 In Tune with Your Dog - John Rogerson
The Northern Centre for Animal Behaviour, 1997.

BOOKS/VIDEOS FOR DOGGY FUN

#1 Take a Bow Wow & Bow Wow Take 2 (2 videos)
Virginia Broitman & Sherri Lippman, Take a Bow Wow, 1995.
(APDT #5, CAPPDT #7)

#2 Agility Tricks - Donna Duford
Clean Run Productions, 1999.

#3 Clicker Fun (3 videos) - Deborah Jones
Canine Training Systems, 1996.

#4 The Trick is in The Training - Stephanie Taunton & Cheryl
Smith. Barron's, 1998.

#5 Fun & Games with Dogs - Roy Hunter
Howlin Moon Press, 1993.

#6 Games People Play... to Train Their Dog (2 booklets)
Terry Ryan, Legacy, 1994.

#7 Canine Adventures - Cynthia Miller
Animalia Publishing Company, 1999.

#8 Fun and Games with Your Dog - Gerd Ludwig
Barron's, 1996.

#9 Dog Tricks: Step by Step - Mary Zeigenfuse & Jan Walker
Howell Book House, 1997.

#10 My Dog Can Do That !
ID Tag Company. 1991. The board game you play with your dog

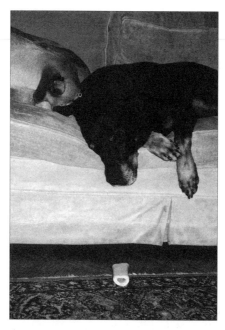

*When dogs are really well-trained, they
can practice couch-work by themselves.
Oliver (left) is still nearly perfect
at seven years of age.
Ivan achieved perfection.
Bless his heart!*

In Memory of
Ivan